HUTCHINSON ENGLISH TEXTS

Selected Poems of
GEORGE HERBERT

HUTCHINSON ENGLISH TEXTS

Selected Poems of George Herbert	Edited by Douglas Brown
Selections from Tennyson	Edited by H. M. Burton
Three Tales from Conrad	Edited by Douglas Brown
W. H. Auden: A Selection	Edited by Richard Hoggart
Viewpoint: An Anthology of Poetry	Edited by Robin Skelton
Andrew Marvell: Some Poems	Edited by James Winny
Anthology of Modern Poetry	Edited by John Wain
Selected Poems of Pope	Edited by Philip Brockbank
A. E. Housman—Poetry and Prose: A Selection	Edited by F. C. Horwood

Selected Poems of
GEORGE HERBERT

with a few representative poems
by his contemporaries

*arranged, with an introduction,
notes, and glossary, by*
DOUGLAS BROWN

HUTCHINSON EDUCATIONAL

HUTCHINSON EDUCATIONAL LTD
3 Fitzroy Square, London W1

London Melbourne Sydney Auckland
Wellington Johannesburg Cape Town
and agencies throughout the world

First published February 1960
Second impression May 1972
Third impression February 1975

Printed in Great Britain by litho by The Anchor Press Ltd
and bound by Wm Brendon & Son Ltd
both of Tiptree, Essex

ISBN 0 09 055920 7

Prefatory Note

I have chosen and arranged these poems of Herbert to serve as an approach, no more: an approach to Herbert's achievement, and through Herbert one possible approach to the nature and achievement of English poetry in the first half of the seventeenth century. The poems have been so grouped as to start on familiar ground, and to lead, by way of an appreciation of his characteristic idiom, to some of the finest examples of that part of his work which can most directly address those who do not share the poet's beliefs—as well as those who do. An appreciation of a few of these poems (the third group in this arrangement) is likely to win from the reader something of that respect, and 'suspension of disbelief', necessary for a profitable approach to the last group.

The introductory material is merely introductory: a short biographical sketch, a look at Herbert through contemporary eyes, and a few very general suggestions about the context in which to read his poems. Readers are invited to go straight from this to their own preliminary study of the poems. That is why the editor's short critical commentary appears after them instead of in the Introduction. The discussion is confined for the most part to undeveloped suggestions, and lines of enquiry; it is intended primarily to stimulate close attention; but it does include a more detailed study of one representative poem from each of the four groups. The notes that follow also seek, in a more random and shorthand way, to direct attention, perhaps to place the weight here rather than there, but not to supply ready-made answers; to engage difficulties but not necessarily to solve them. The glossary, on the other hand, is intended to go some way at least towards answers and solutions. Herbert works so skilfully and knowingly with the deep grain of our language, that readers are advised to be continually wary about his words, and to consult either the glossary or a good dictionary frequently. One can very well manage without editorial criticism and notes, and so much the better; but with poetry of this time and tradition, it is safe to say, one cannot manage without a dictionary.

The double conviction, that a poet cannot be well studied in isolation from his best contemporaries, and that Herbert's poetry can serve admirably as an approach to a wider and deeper study of 'metaphysical poetry' generally, has led me to include with each group of Herbert's poems two or three representative and comparable poems by others: those from whom he learnt, those whom his own poetry affected, and those among his peers whose related, but different, work can begin to make us really conscious of a 'tradition'. With the equivocal exception of the last poem in the book, however, choice from the poetry of Herbert's contemporaries has been confined to what they would have called 'divine poems'; some principle of selection was necessary, and the adoption of this principle may make comparative reading more profitable.

Some of the most helpful and suggestive insights from published criticism of Herbert have been quoted in the notes on certain poems. I had in mind that particular perceptions about particular poems are more germane to real appreciation than paragraphs and passages excerpted and quoted *en bloc* as 'what the critics say' and thus given a rather weighty and dogmatic prestige. I have been directed and assisted in many ways, both over the years and in the preparation of this edition, by published work on Herbert and his contemporaries. The suggestions for further reading at the end of the notes will indicate some of my sources. I wish, though, to acknowledge a special debt to Canon Hutchinson's edition of Herbert's *Works*.

D. B.

Contents

Prefatory note   5

Introduction
   A short biographical portrait   11
   Early records   16
   The social and literary setting   22

I HYMNS AND ANTHEMS

Praise (II)   29
Antiphon (I)   30
Vertue   31
The Elixir   32
The 23d Psalme   33

Philip Sidney's *Psalm XXIII*   34
Robert Southwell's *New Prince, New Pompe*   35
Henry Vaughan's *Peace*   37

II HIS QUICK-PIERCING MIND

Deniall   41
Jordan (I)   42
The Quip   43

Dialogue	44
Giddinesse	45
Redemption	46
Hope	47
Sinnes Round	48
Jordan (II)	49
Love (III)	50
Thomas Carew's *Lines for Maria Wentworth*	51
John Donne's *Holy Sonnet X*	52
Henry Vaughan's *The Morning-Watch*	53

III THE MANY SPIRITUAL CONFLICTS

The Collar	57
The Crosse	59
Confession	61
Conscience	62
Affliction (I)	63
Affliction (IV)	66
The Pearl	68
The Flower	70
The Pilgrimage	72
John Donne's *A Hymne to God the Father*	74
Andrew Marvell's *A Dialogue between the Soul and Body*	75

IV POETRY OF MEDITATION

Aaron	79
The Pulley	80

Prayer (II)	81
The Agonie	82
The Sacrifice	83
Henry King's *The Exequy*	93
John Donne's *Goodfriday, 1613: Riding Westward*	97
Andrew Marvell's *To his Coy Mistress*	99
Critical commentary and notes	101
Suggestions for further reading	151
Glossary	153

INTRODUCTION

A short biographical portrait

'*Of noble birth*'

George Herbert was born in 1593, in Montgomery. He was the fifth son of Richard and Magdelen Herbert, of an ancient aristocratic family long distinguished in public life, proud and ambitious. His elder brother Edward, Lord Herbert of Cherbury, achieved the greater contemporary fame; and he was the more typical of the family—courtier, diplomat, poet, philosopher, writer. His father died when George Herbert was three, and his widowed mother, the remarkable Lady Magdelen Herbert, devoted herself to the education and guidance of her children. She was a lady of the finest intelligence, sensitive and perceptive, a devoted Christian, the admired friend of such eminent men as Dr. John Donne the poet and preacher. George Herbert has left his own record of the care and order of his mother's style of life; her practical charity; her love of music, of serious conversation and correspondence; and also her love to her family, and her severity in directing their paths. The boy was educated at Westminster School, whose reputation for classical studies stood particularly high. He was already a scholar marked out for distinction when he went up to Trinity College, Cambridge, at the age of seventeen.

'*The excellent endowments of his minde*'

At the university he quickly distinguished himself. He became a Fellow of Trinity and a college lecturer. His studies were in classics and divinity equally, in rhetoric, and in Latin and English verse. It seems that his mother had early prepared him for the vocation of holy orders, but from this step periodically his nature drew back; not that he diminished his allegiance to the Church, or his studies in theology. From a resolve early expressed in two sonnets he sent his mother, to dedicate his skill in language to the pursuit of sacred poetry, however, he never drew back. During the Cambridge years he composed many of the first drafts of poems later to take their place in his one volume of poetry, *The Temple*, published after his death. These poems circulated, as was usual, in manuscript, and Herbert's reputation began to grow, both in Cambridge and in the court circles of London: he became known as a poet and an intellectual, as a lecturer and a wit. He was good-looking, and graced with attractive manners. His high birth, his fine presence, and his brilliance of mind combined to advance him in the world. But he began, even so early, to suffer from ill-health and consequent periods of despondency. He lived well, not without some vanity and ostentation, especially in dress; a sense of his own unusual powers combined with the drives of ambition native to his family. He seems at this time not to have been troubled by any sense of discrepancy between the claims of his faith and the possibilities of greatness in the world. From his first university office of Reader in Rhetoric, he aspired to become Public Orator for the sake of the prestige of that office, and the likelihood of advancing through it towards eventual civil power. To a friend's comment that 'this place, being civil, may divert me too much from Divinity, at which not without cause he thinks I aim', his response was to detect 'no such earthiness' in the office, 'but it may very well be joyn'd with Heaven'. He used every influence he could command to secure the office, and in 1620 he did secure it.

'A laudible ambition to be something more than he then was'

He remained Public Orator in Cambridge University for seven years, but for the last three or four of those years he was infrequently at Cambridge, bent rather upon court preferment in London. We do not know, and can only conjecture, the vacillations, tensions perhaps, that he experienced between the call of holy orders and the new opportunities for power and place apparent to him. But by the time of King James's death in 1625 the lure of public distinction and power had lost its hold upon him. He had stood high in the King's favour, although family and parliamentary dissensions in which he was involved placed him in an equivocal position; more so with King Charles, although his court was more serious and better conducted, and more likely to command Herbert's real allegiance. His distinguished brother was temporarily under a cloud in court circles, and he seems to have become disillusioned with the political world through his membership of Parliament and his increasing insight into court ways. The terrible plague in London may have had some deep effect upon him; so, even more, may the retirement from 'the world' of his friend Nicholas Ferrar, who was ordained deacon, and withdrew with his family to Little Gidding. Probably behind all these sources of unease was a loss of that earlier conviction that divinity and civil power could be joined so naturally; an increasing doubt of the ideal he had held, of union between Church and State in high affairs.

However these and other causes may have worked upon him, Herbert went into retirement for a while, and made a resolve for holy orders. In 1626 he was ordained deacon, and accepted some minor offices in the Church that did not commit him to parochial life. It was a decisive step to have taken for a man of his high birth, who had attained to such eminence as he had. It debarred him from further civil advancement. There is little doubt that Dr. John Donne, now Dean of St. Paul's, who had passed through conflicts of his own and who was much with Herbert during a part of his retirement, encouraged and advised him. His mother was near the end of her life, in poor health and given to melancholy, and this, too, probably affected her son's decision. Ill-health continued to take its toll of him. 'About the 34th year of his Age,' Walton reports, 'Mr. Herbert was seized with a sharp

quotidian Ague, and thought to remove it by a change of air.'
He continued to live in retirement as a private gentleman, to
build up his health and to dispose his heart finally towards the
obscure and modest life of a parish priest. 'He had heard sober
men censure him,' said a contemporary, 'as a man that did not
manage his brave parts to his best advantage and preferment, but
lost himself in an humble way.' Inevitably a man of such innate
pride and such endowments of mind and personality as Herbert
found difficulty in reconciling himself to such a verdict. He had
always been given to self-searching, and even in his earlier
university years was subject to periods of despondency and
uncertain mood. His instincts and temperament, 'not exempt
from passion and choler', could not be easily subdued to the
simple and exemplary calling to which he now aspired. To these
years many of the poems in *The Temple* reflecting inner division
probably belong. He was held back from accepting a parish both
by a sense of unworthiness, and by that absolute allegiance to the
tenets of his Faith and Church which made him 'apprehensive
of the last great Account that he was to make for the Cure of so
many souls'. His health recovered; he married Jane Danvers,
a lady of one of the great Wiltshire families, who thus shared
with him the 'losing himself in an humble way', and in 1630
accepted the living of Bemerton, near Salisbury.

'The great sanctity of the short remainder of his holy life'

The two churches at Bemerton were small, undistinguished, and
(like the rectory itself) in need of repair. Out of his own means,
Herbert restored all three; he made a home for the orphaned
daughters of his sister Margaret Vaughan; he became chaplain to
the Earl of Pembroke and his countess; and he maintained a
curate. Once he had accepted its full implications, Herbert's
dedication to his calling became almost legendary. Such tributes
as that of his friend Ferrar, which was published as preface to
The Temple and appeared only one year after his death, sufficiently attest the facts of his sanctity and reputation. 'His life,'

wrote his more famous brother, 'was most holy and exemplary; insomuch that about Salisbury, where he lived, beneficed for many years, he was little less than sainted.' His inward conflicts seem to have been much quieted when he went to Bemerton, but echoes remained and neither ill-health nor those varying moods of despondency left him undisturbed for long. More than half the poems of *The Temple* were composed during the three years of his rectory at Bemerton; he used the poet's art not only as a means to consecrate his praise and devotion, but also to clarify and resolve the tensions within that passionate and complex personality of his; and again (as Canon Hutchinson suggests), to offer a defence against pain and weakness, by making music of his suffering and disappointment. That he entrusted his book of poems to his dearest friend, Nicholas Ferrar, when he felt the approach of death, shows what value he set upon his poetry. He continued to study and to compose extensively (not all his writings survived), and 'to give himself a mark to aim at' he wrote *A Priest to the Temple, or The Country Parson, His Character and Rule of Holy Life*, a practical manual of the priestly life in a small parish.

Twice daily he said the offices in his little church. He seems indeed to have been, to his parishioners, the exemplar of the priest's life that he sought to become: accessible to all, tender to the impoverished and unhappy, a sensitive friend and yet a stern guide, seriously assuming the responsibility for the souls of all in his charge. It was an achievement of character; for the poems, and all other evidences, suggest that he remained, within, the turbulent and passionate spirit of earlier years, a true descendant of the Herbert clan. After only three years of ministry, illness and bodily weakness set increasing limits to his pastoral activity. He died in 1632, of consumption, at the age of forty.

II Early records

Passages from Walton's 'Life'

... In that year he was also made *Master of Arts*, he being then in the 22nd year of his Age; during all which time, all, or the greatest diversion from his Study, was the practice of Musick, in which he became a great Master; and of which, he would say, 'That it did relieve his drooping spirits, compose his distracted thoughts, and raised his weary soul so far above Earth, that it gave him an earnest of the joys of Heaven, before he possest them.' And it may be noted, that from his first entrance into the Colledge, the generous Dr. *Nevil* was a cherisher of his Studies, and such a lover of his person, his behaviour, and the excellent endowments of his mind, that he took him often into his own company; by which he confirm'd his native gentileness; and, if during this time he expresst any Error, it was, that he kept himself too much retir'd, and at too great a distance with all his inferiours: and his cloaths seem'd to prove, that he put too great a value on his parts and Parentage. . . .

... In this place of *Orator* our *George Herbert* continued eight years; and manag'd it with as becoming, and grave a gaiety, as any had ever before, or since his time. For He had acquir'd great Learning, and was blest with a high fancy, a civil and sharp wit, and with a natural elegance, both in his behaviour, his tongue, and his pen. . . .

... In this time of being *Orator*, he had learnt to understand the *Italian*, *Spanish*, and *French* Tongues very perfectly; hoping, that as his Predecessors, so he might in time attain the place of a *Secretary of State*, he being at that time very high in the Kings favour; and not meanly valued and lov'd by the most eminent and most powerful of the Court-Nobility: This, and the love of a Court-conversation mixt with a laudable ambition to be something more than he then was, drew him often from *Cambridge* to attend the *King* wheresoever the Court was, who then gave him a *Sine Cure*, which fell into his Majesties disposal, I think, by the death of the Bishop of St. *Asaph*. It was the same, that Queen *Elizabeth* had formerly given to her Favourite Sir *Philip Sidney*; and valued to be worth an hundred and twenty pound *per Annum*. With this, and his Annuity, and the advantage of his Colledge, and of his Oratorship, he enjoyed his gentile humour for cloaths, and Court-like company, and seldom look'd towards *Cambridge*, unless the King were there, but then he never fail'd....

... When at his Induction he was shut into *Bemerton* Church, being left there alone to Toll the Bell (as the Law requires him:) he staid so much longer than an ordinary time, before he return'd to those Friends that staid expecting him at the Church-door, that his Friend, Mr. *Woodnot*, look'd in at the Church-window, and saw him lie prostrate on the ground before the Altar: at which time and place (as he after told Mr. *Woodnot*) he set some Rules to himself, for the future manage of his life; and then and there made a vow, to labour to keep them....

... And by this account of his diligence, to make his Parishioners understand what they pray'd, and why they prais'd, and ador'd their Creator: I hope I shall the more easily obtain the Readers belief to the following account of Mr. *Herberts* own practice; which was, to appear constantly with his Wife, and three Neeces (the daughters of a deceased Sister) and his whole Family, twice every day at the Church-prayers, in the Chappel which does almost joyn to his Parsonage-house. And for the time of his appearing, it was strictly at the Canonical hours of 10 and 4; and then and there, he lifted up pure and charitable hands to God in the midst of the Congregation. And he would joy to have spent that time in that place, where the honour of his *Master Jesus* dwelleth; and there, by that inward devotion which he testified constantly by an humble behaviour, and visible adoration, he, like *Josua* brought not only *his own Household thus to serve the Lord*; but brought most of his Parishioners, and many Gentlemen in the Neighbourhood, constantly to make a part of his Congregation twice a day; and some of the meaner sort of his Parish, did so love and reverence Mr. *Herbert*, that they would let their Plow rest when Mr. *Herberts Saints-Bell* rung to Prayers, that they might also offer their devotions to God with him: and would then return back to their Plow. And his most holy life was such, that it begot such reverence to God, and to him, that they thought themselves the happier, when they carried Mr. *Herberts* blessing back with them to their labour.—Thus powerful was his reason, and example, to perswade others to a practical piety, and devotion. . . .

. . . His chiefest recreation was Musick, in which heavenly Art he was a most excellent Master, and did himself compose many *divine Hymns* and *Anthems*, which he set and sung to his *Lute* or *Viol*; and though he was a lover of retiredness, yet his love to *Musick* was such, that he went usually twice every week on certain appointed days, to the *Cathedral Church* in *Salisbury*; and at his return would say, *That his time spent in Prayer, and Cathedral Musick, elevated his Soul, and was his Heaven upon Earth:* But before his return thence to *Bemerton*, he would usually sing and play his part, at an appointed private Musick-meeting; and, to justifie this practice, he would often say, *Religion does not banish Mirth, but only moderates, and sets rules to it.* . . .

. . . In another walk to *Salisbury*, he saw a poor man, with a poorer horse, that was fall'n under his Load; they were both in distress, and needed present help; which Mr. *Herbert* perceiving, put off his Canonical Coat, and help'd the poor man to unload, and after, to load his horse: The poor man blest him for it: and he blest the poor man; and was so like the *good Samaritan*, that he gave him money to refresh both himself and his horse; and told him, *That if he lov'd himself he should be merciful to his Beast.*— Thus he left the poor man, and at his coming to his musical friends at *Salisbury*, they began to wonder that Mr. *George Herbert* which us'd to be so trim and clean, came into that company so soyl'd and discompos'd; but he told them the occasion: And when one of the company told him, *He had disparag'd himself by so dirty an employment;* his answer was, *That the thought of what he had done, would prove Musick to him at Midnight; and that the omission of it, would have upbraided and made discord in his Conscience, whensoever he should pass by that place; for, if I be bound to pray for all that be in distress, I am sure that I am bound so far as it is in my power to practise what I pray for. And though I do not wish for the like occasion every day, yet let me tell you, I would not willingly pass one day of my life without comforting a sad soul, or shewing mercy; and I praise God for this occasion*: And now let's tune our Instruments. . . .

. . . Mr. *Duncon*, according to his promise, return'd from *Bath* the fifth day, and then found Mr. *Herbert* much weaker than he left him: and therefore their Discourse could not be long; but at Mr. *Duncons* parting with him, Mr. *Herbert* spoke to this purpose—*Sir, I pray give my brother* Farrer *an account of the decaying condition of my body, and tell him, I beg him to continue his daily prayers for me: and let him know, that I have consider'd,* That God only is what he would bee; *and that I am by his grace become now so like him, as to be pleas'd with what pleaseth him; and tell him, that I do not repine but am pleas'd with my want of health; and tell him, my heart is fixt on that place where true joy is only to be found; and that I long to be there, and do wait for my appointed change with* hope *and* patience. Having said this, he did with so sweet a humility as seem'd to exalt him, bow down to Mr. *Duncon*, and with a thoughtful and contented look, say to him,—*Sir, I pray deliver this little Book to my dear brother* Farrer, *and tell him, he shall find in it a picture of the many spiritual Conflicts that have past betwixt God and my Soul, before I could subject mine to the will of* Jesus *my*

Master: *in whose service I have now found perfect freedom; desire him to read it; and then, if he can think it may turn to the advantage of any dejected poor Soul, let it be made Publick: if not, let him burn it: for I and it, are less than the least of God's mercies.*—Thus meanly did this humble man think of this excellent Book, which now bears the name of *The TEMPLE:* Or, *Sacred Poems,* and *Private Ejaculations*; of which, Mr. *Farrer* would say, *There was in it the picture of a divine Soul in every page; and that the whole Book was such a harmony of Holy passions, as would enrich the World with pleasure and piety.* And it appears to have done so: for there have been more than Twenty thousand of them sold since the first Impression. . . .

From Ferrar's Preface to '*The Temple*'

The dedication of this work having been made by the Authour to the *Divine Majestie* onely, how should we now presume to interest any mortall man in the patronage of it? Much lesse think we it meet to seek the recommendation of the Muses, for that which himself was confident to have been inspired by a diviner breath then flows from *Helicon*. The world therefore shall receive it in that naked simplicitie, with which he left it, without any addition either of support or ornament, more then is included in it self. We leave it free and unforestalled to every mans judgement, and to the benefit that he shall find by perusall. Onely for the clearing of some passages, we have thought it not unfit to make the common Reader privie to some few particularities of the condition and disposition of the Person;

Being nobly born, and as eminently endued with gifts of the minde, and having by industrie and happy education perfected them to that great height of excellencie, whereof his fellowship of Trinitie Colledge in Cambridge, and his Orator-ship in the Universitie, together with that knowledge which the Kings Court had taken of him, could make relation farre above ordinarie. Quitting both his deserts and all the opportunities that he had for worldly preferment, he betook himself to the Sanctuarie and Temple of God, choosing rather to serve at Gods Altar, then to seek the honour of State-employments. As for those inward enforcements to this course (for outward there was none) which many of these ensuing verses bear witness of, they detract not from the freedome, but adde to the honour of this resolution in him. As God had enabled him, so he accounted him meet not onely to be called, but to be compelled to this service: Wherein his faithfull discharge was such, as may make him justly a companion to the primitive Saints, and a pattern or more for the age he lived in.

To testifie his independencie upon all others, and to quicken his diligence in this kinde, he used in his ordinarie speech, when he made mention of the blessed name of our Lord and Saviour Jesus Christ, to adde, *My Master*. . . .

III A brief note on the social and literary setting

A glance through the biographical portrait, and a savouring of Walton's and Ferrar's reports, will give the reader a sufficient feeling for Herbert's times to enable the poetry to speak more clearly. The court at London is the hub of English life, the focus of every kind of art and literature, as well as of political energy and intrigue. The King's sovereignty is still real, and the power of the old nobility and their cultural responsibilities are real also; but far-reaching economic changes have transferred wealth to merchant adventurers and city speculators, and aristocratic power is no longer impregnable. The Church of England, accommodating the double claims of puritanism and the old catholic tradition, is both a spiritual and a secular force in the land, and some part of both those traditions can be seen affecting such men as Herbert. Religion is still a paramount concern in all walks of life: but in university and city circles, the new Learning, the spirit of sceptical inquiry, the energetic delight in intellectual adventure, have modified the older patterns of theology and belief and loosened many bonds; so, in other ways, have such factors as the increasing interest in self-analysis, the deeper and sharper self-consciousness prevalent among the highly educated, the cult of melancholy, and the economic uncertainties of the time. To compose and read poetry is still an educated nobleman's expected skill and pleasure: Lord Herbert of Cherbury, combining diplomacy, philosophy and poetry, and achieving distinction in all three, is eminent but characteristic. Poems circulate in manuscript within a fairly small élite drawn from city, university, and court. Distinction of mind, wit and verbal skill, and intellectual rigour in conversation and writing, are admired. A common education, a common training in rhetoric—the skills of speech for argument, persuasion, and expression—bind together this select circle of readers, writers, thinkers and talkers. Herbert's own training and high repute in rhetoric, in the forms and styles of composition, are something his public appreciates and admires.

That is one of the first points to take about the literary setting for these poems: Herbert's verse is that of a consummate rhetorician. Its sharp wit, and evident delight in the free play of the mind, derive partly from the court and university environment; but much more from the new style and fashion in love poetry and divine poetry, whose presiding genius was John Donne. Whether the apparent subject be flippant or highly serious, an energetic intellectual passion distinguishes this style; 'the intellect is at the tips of the senses', mental dexterity fuses with nervous excitement or with feelings of sight, hearing, smell. As a result, a new and wider range of human experiences becomes material for poetic art, for illumination by image, by emblem, or by logical analogue. The mind's interests, particularly, become the very stuff of poetry: hence (in part) the application of the general term 'metaphysical poetry' to the style Donne inaugurates and Herbert, in his own way, delights in.

But delight in paradox and irony, and dexterous analogies, had long had a place in the Christian tradition; it was a way of discerning the central Christian truths themselves. Donne—and much more, Herbert—are not altogether innovators here; their divine poetry has to be read against a background of sacred commentary, of catholic liturgy, and the achievement of an earlier poet like Southwell. And immediately behind another facet of the 'new style' is something even more significant: the great age of English drama, of dramatic blank verse. Herbert's age is the age of Shakespeare; the Shakespearean mode, and the language of the London stage, contribute the most powerful backing to that most lively power of the metaphysicals—their subtle mastery of the rhythms in all the varieties of human speech, their skill in playing off the colloquial impetus of the voice against a formal metrical pattern. Another influential figure should be named here who in his person unites the art of poetic drama with the art of lyric poetry: Ben Jonson. He exercised upon the attitudes poets took up towards their subjects, and upon the skills of versification, an influence out of proportion to his own achievement in lyric poetry—vigorous and incisive though that is. He established a direction complementary to that pioneered by Donne, towards classical refinement and terse exactitude, towards a blending of sharply pointed and racy speech with graceful forms and a genial yet cultivated manner. How well Herbert's accomplishment fits this mould, too, will easily become apparent; but a poet of an older generation who was in some sense predecessor to Jonson himself in all this, affected Herbert more intimately: Sir Philip Sidney. In his love poems there is the more lavish and studied eloquence of the Elizabethan manner. But the way natural, personal relationships, sensitive earnestness and direct self-giving blend with conventional forms and rhetorical devices, makes a significant preparation for Herbert's poetry. There is the disconcerting fusion of logical subtlety and dexterity with honesty and tenderness, in the best of Sidney, that we may wrongly think of as peculiarly Herbert's. And if Sidney's secular sonnets to Stella indicate this much, his divine poems—notably the metrical versions of the first forty psalms—come even nearer to those we are to study.

The love poems and psalms of Sidney; the poems of Southwell; the lyrics of Ben Jonson; the verse of the Elizabethan stage—these need all to be set alongside Donne's achievement, in a picture of Herbert's inheritance. Two other aspects of that inheritance deserve a short reference. First, the widespread and ingenious Elizabethan cultivation of the arts of song and of verse for music persisted into Herbert's age. He was a musician himself, and composed much for singing (the poems in this selection start there); both in verses for music, and in his poetry at large, the concern for metrical variety, for decisive progression from stanza to stanza, for the stable underlying form habitual in composition for song, may be detected. Second, and the more so because we may find something unsympathetic or uncongenial here, we need to recall the prevalence in Herbert's time of ways of thought, reflection, and devotion, based upon emblems and symbols and figures and types. The appeal of allegory was still very much alive, the instinctive perception of analogies and comparisons; and the conviction that these meanings really were *there* to be perceived, were there by divine purpose. Spenser's *Faerie Queene*, we should remind ourselves, achieved its fame during Herbert's boyhood. Bunyan's *Pilgrim's Progress* achieved its fame some thirty years after his death. Into this habit of mind and imagination, flexible and quick to grasp similitudes and the 'point' of a comparison, to grasp the *representative* character of a plight or situation, or the 'picture' behind formal references, we have now to try to enter.

I

Hymns and Anthems

'His chiefest recreation was Musick, in which heavenly Art he was a most excellent Master, and did himself compose many divine Hymns and Anthems, which he set and sung to his Lute or Viol. . . .'

Walton's 'Life'

Praise (II)

King of Glorie, King of Peace,
        I will love thee:
And that love may never cease,
        I will move thee.

Thou hast granted my request,
        Thou hast heard me:
Thou didst note my working breast,
        Thou hast spar'd me.

Wherefore with my utmost art
        I will sing thee,
And the cream of all my heart
        I will bring thee.

Though my sinnes against me cried,
        Thou didst cleare me;
And alone, when they replied,
        Thou didst heare me.

Sev'n whole dayes, not one in seven,
        I will praise thee.
In my heart, though not in heaven,
        I can raise thee.

Thou grew'st soft and moist with tears,
        Thou relentedst:
And when Justice call'd for fears
        Thou dissentedst.

Small it is, in this poore sort
        To enroll thee:
Ev'n eternitie is too short
        To extoll thee.

Antiphon (I)

set apart
antiphonal
↓
Heaven / Earth
Church / Heart

Cho. Let all the world in ev'ry corner sing,
   My God and King.

Vers. The heav'ns are not too high,
   His praise may thither flie:
   The earth is not too low,
   His praises there may grow.

Cho. Let all the world in ev'ry corner sing,
   My God and King.

heart set
in contradistinction
to Church.

Vers. The church with psalms must shout,
   No doore can keep them out:
   But above all, the heart
   Must bear the longest part.

Cho. Let all the world in ev'ry corner sing,
   My God and King.

The beauty of holiness

Vertue

Sweet day, so cool, so calm, so bright,
The bridall of the earth and skie:
The dew shall weep thy fall to night;
        For thou must die.

Sweet rose, whose hue angrie and brave
Bids the rash gazer wipe his eye:
Thy root is ever in its grave,
        And thou must die.

Sweet spring, full of sweet dayes and roses,
A box where sweets compacted lie;
My musick shows ye have your closes,
        And all must die.

Onely a sweet and vertuous soul,
Like season'd timber, never gives;
But though the whole world turn to coal,
        Then chiefly lives.

The Elixir

Teach me, my God and King,
In all things thee to see,
And what I do in any thing,
To do it as for thee:

Not rudely, as a beast,
To runne into an action;
But still to make thee prepossest,
And give it his perfection.

A man that looks on glasse
On it may stay his eye;
Or if he pleaseth, through it passe,
And then the heav'n espie.

All may of thee partake:
Nothing can be so mean,
Which with his tincture (for thy sake)
Will not grow bright and clean.

A servant with this clause
Makes drudgerie divine:
Who sweeps a room, as for thy laws,
Makes that and th'action fine.

This is the famous stone
That turneth all to gold:
For that which God doth touch and own
Cannot for lesse be told.

The 23d Psalme

The God of love my shepherd is,
    And he that doth me feed:
While he is mine, and I am his,
    What can I want or need?

He leads me to the tender grasse,
    Where I both feed and rest;
Then to the streams that gently passe:
    In both I have the best.

Or if I stray, he doth convert
    And bring my mind in frame:
And all this not for my desert,
    But for his holy name.

Yea, in deaths shadie black abode
    Well may I walk, not fear:
For thou art with me; and thy rod
    To guide, thy staffe to bear.

Nay, thou dost make me sit and dine,
    Ev'n in my enemies sight:
My head with oyl, my cup with wine
    Runnes over day and night.

Surely thy sweet and wondrous love
    Shall measure all my dayes;
And as it never shall remove,
    So neither shall my praise.

SIR PHILIP SIDNEY

Psalm XXIII

The Lord, the Lord my Shepheard is,
    And so can never I
        Tast missery.
He rests me in greene pasture his:
    By waters still and sweete
        He guides my feete.

Hee me revives; leades me the way,
    Which righteousness doth take,
        For his name sake.
Yea, though I should through valleys stray
    Of deathes dark shade, I will
        Noe whitt feare ill.

For thou, deare Lord, thou me besett'st;
    Thy rodd and thy staff be
        To comfort me:
Before me thou a table sett'st,
    Even when foes envious eye
        Doth it espy.

Thou oil'st my head, thou fill'st my cupp,
    Nay, more, thou endlesse good,
        Shalt give me food.
To thee, I say, ascended up,
    Where thou, the Lord of all,
        Dost hold thy hall.

ROBERT SOUTHWELL

New Prince, New Pompe

Behold a silly tender Babe
   In freezing Winter night,
In homely Manger trembling lyes;
   Alas a pitious sight:

The Innes are full, no man will yield
   This little Pilgrime bed;
But forc't he is with silly beasts,
   In Crib to shrowd his head.

Despise him not for lying there:
   First what he is enquire:
An orient pearle is often found
   In depth of dirtie mire.

Waigh not his Crib, his woodden dish
   Nor beasts that by him feed:
Waigh not his Mother's poore attire,
   Nor *Iosephs* simple weed.

This Stable is a Princes Court,
   The Crib his chaire of State:
The Beasts are parcell of his Pompe,
   The woodden dish his plate.

The persons, in that poore attire,
   His royall liveries weare,
The Prince himselfe is com'n from heaven,
   This pompe is prized there.

With joy approach, O Christian wight,
　Doe homage to thy King;
And highly prayse his humble Pompe,
　Which He from Heaven doth bring.

HENRY VAUGHAN

Peace

My Soul, there is a Countrie
    Far beyond the stars,
Where stands a winged Centrie
    All skilfull in the wars,
There above noise, and danger
    Sweet peace sits crown'd with smiles,
And One born in a Manger
    Commands the Beauteous files,
He is thy gracious friend,
    And (O my Soul awake!)
Did in pure love descend
    To die here for thy sake,
If thou canst get but thither,
    There grows the flowre of peace,
The Rose that cannot wither,
    Thy fortresse, and thy ease;
Leave then thy foolish ranges;
    For none can thee secure,
But one, who never changes,
    Thy God, thy life, thy Cure.

II

His Quick-piercing Mind

'... dipping and seasoning all our words and sentences in our hearts before they come into our mouths, truly affecting and cordially expressing all that we say; so that the auditors may plainly perceive that every word is heart-deep....'

Herbert's 'Country Parson'

Deniall

When my devotions could not pierce
    Thy silent eares;
Then was my heart broken, as was my verse:
    My breast was full of fears
        And disorder:

My bent thoughts, like a brittle bow,
    Did flie asunder:
Each took his way; some would to pleasures go,
    Some to the warres and thunder
        Of alarms.

As good go any where, they say,
    As to benumme
Both knees and heart, in crying night and day,
    Come, come, my God, O come,
        But no hearing.

O that thou shouldst give dust a tongue
    To crie to thee,
And then not heare it crying! all day long
    My heart was in my knee,
        But no hearing.

Therefore my soul lay out of sight,
    Untun'd, unstrung:
My feeble spirit, unable to look right,
    Like a nipt blossome, hung
        Discontented.

O cheer and tune my heartlesse breast,
    Deferre no time;
That so thy favours granting my request
    They and my minde may chime,
        And mend my ryme.

Jordan (I)

Who sayes that fictions onely and false hair
Become a verse? Is there in truth no beautie?
Is all good structure in a winding stair?
May no lines passe, except they do their dutie
    Not to a true, but painted chair?

Is it no verse, except enchanted groves
And sudden arbours shadow course-spunne lines?
Must purling streams refresh a lovers loves?
Must all be vail'd, while he that reades, divines,
    Catching the sense at two removes?

Shepherds are honest people; let them sing:
Riddle who list, for me, and pull for Prime:
I envie no mans nightingale or spring;
Nor let them punish me with loss of rime,
    Who plainly say, *My God, My King*.

The Quip

The merrie world did on a day
With his train-bands and mates agree
To meet together, where I lay,
And all in sport to geere at me.

First, Beautie crept into a rose,
Which when I pluckt not, Sir, said she,
Tell me, I pray, Whose hands are those?
But thou shalt answer, Lord, for me.

Then Money came, and chinking still,
What tune is this, poore man? said he:
I heard in Musick you had skill.
But thou shalt answer, Lord, for me.

Then came brave Glorie puffing by
In silks that whistled, who but he?
He scarce allow'd me half an eie.
But thou shalt answer, Lord, for me.

Then came quick Wit and Conversation,
And he would needs a comfort be,
And, to be short, make an Oration.
But thou shalt answer, Lord, for me.

Yet when the houre of thy designe
To answer these fine things shall come;
Speak not at large; say, I am thine:
And then they have their answer home.

Dialogue

Sweetest Saviour, if my soul
    Were but worth the having,
Quickly should I then controll
    Any thought of waving.
But when all my care and pains
Cannot give the name of gains
To thy wretch so full of stains,
What delight or hope remains?

What, Child, is the ballance thine,
    Thine the poise and measure?
If I say, Thou shalt be mine;
    Finger not my treasure.
What the gains in having thee
Do amount to, onely he,
Who for man was sold, can see;
That transferr'd th'accounts to me.

But as I can see no merit,
    Leading to this favour:
So the way to fit me for it
    Is beyond my savour.
As the reason then is thine;
So the way is none of mine:
I disclaim the whole designe:
Sinne disclaims and I resigne.

That is all, if that I could
    Get without repining;
And my clay, my creature, would
    Follow my resigning:
That as I did freely part
With my glorie and desert,
Left all joyes to feel all smart—
    Ah! no more: thou break'st my heart.

Giddinesse

Oh, what a thing is man! how farre from power,
    From settled peace and rest!
He is some twentie sev'rall men at least
    Each sev'rall houre.

One while he counts of heav'n, as of his treasure:
    But then a thought creeps in,
And calls him coward, who for fear of sinne
    Will lose a pleasure.

Now he will fight it out, and to the warres;
    Now eat his bread in peace,
And snudge in quiet: now he scorns increase;
    Now all day spares.

He builds a house, which quickly down must go,
    As if a whirlwinde blew
And crusht the building: and it's partly true,
    His minde is so.

O what a sight were Man, if his attires
    Did alter with his minde;
And like a Dolphins skinne, his clothes combin'd
    With his desires!

Surely if each one saw anothers heart,
    There would be no commerce,
No sale or bargain passe: all would disperse,
    And live apart.

Lord, mend or rather make us: one creation
    Will not suffice our turn:
Except thou make us dayly, we shall spurn
    Our own salvation.

Redemption

Having been tenant long to a rich Lord
    Not thriving, I resolved to be bold,
    And make a suit unto him, to afford
A new small-rented lease, and cancell th'old.
In heaven at his manour I him sought:
    They told me there, that he was lately gone
    About some land, which he had dearly bought
Long since on earth, to take possession.
I straight return'd, and knowing his great birth,
    Sought him accordingly in great resorts;
    In cities, theatres, gardens, parks, and courts:
At length I heard a ragged noise and mirth
    Of theeves and murderers: there I him espied,
    Who straight, *Your suit is granted*, said, & died.

Hope

I gave to Hope a watch of mine: but he
        An anchor gave to me.
Then an old prayer-book I did present:
        And he an optick sent.
With that I gave a viall full of tears:
        But he a few green eares.
Ah Loyterer! I'le no more, no more I'le bring:
        I did expect a ring.

Sinnes Round

Sorrie I am, my God, sorrie I am,
That my offences course it in a ring.
My thoughts are working like a busie flame,
Untill their cockatrice they hatch and bring:
And when they once have perfected their draughts,
My words take fire from my inflamed thoughts.

My words take fire from my inflamed thoughts,
Which spit it forth like the Sicilian Hill.
They vent the wares, and passe them with their faults,
And by their breathing ventilate the ill.
But words suffice not, where are lewd intentions:
My hands do joyn to finish the inventions.

My hands do joyn to finish the inventions:
And so my sinnes ascend three stories high,
As Babel grew, before there were dissensions.
Yet ill deeds loyter not: for they supplie
New thoughts of sinning: wherefore, to my shame,
Sorrie I am, my God, sorrie I am.

Jordan (II)

When first my lines of heavn'ly joyes made mention,
Such was their lustre, they did so excell,
That I sought out quaint words, and trim invention;
My thoughts began to burnish, sprout, and swell,
Curling with metaphors a plain intention,
Decking the sense, as if it were to sell.

Thousands of notions in my brain did runne,
Off'ring their service, if I were not sped:
I often blotted what I had begunne;
This was not quick enough, and that was dead.
Nothing could seem too rich to clothe the sunne,
Much lesse those joyes which trample on his head.

As flames do work and winde, when they ascend,
So did I weave my self into the sense.
But while I bustled, I might heare a friend
Whisper, *How wide is all this long pretence!*
There is in love a sweetnesse readie penn'd:
Copie out onely that, and save expense.

Love (III)

Love bade me welcome: yet my soul drew back,
        Guiltie of dust and sinne.
But quick-ey'd Love, observing me grow slack
        From my first entrance in,
Drew nearer to me, sweetly questioning,
        If I lack'd any thing.

A guest, I answer'd, worthy to be here:
        Love said, You shall be he.
I the unkinde, ungratefull? Ah my deare,
        I cannot look on thee.
Love took my hand, and smiling did reply,
        Who made the eyes but I?

Truth Lord, but I have marr'd them: let my shame
        Go where it doth deserve.
And know you not, sayes Love, who bore the blame?
        My deare, then I will serve.
You must sit down, sayes Love, and taste my meat:
        So I did sit and eat.

THOMAS CAREW

Lines for Maria Wentworth

And here the precious dust is layd;
Whose purely temper'd Clay was made
So fine, that it the guest betray'd.

Else the soule grew so fast within,
It broke the outward shell of sinne,
And so was hatch'd a Cherubin.

In heigth, it soar'd to God above;
In depth, it did to knowledge move,
And spread in breadth to generall love.

Before, a pious duty shind
To Parents, courtesie behind,
On either side an equall mind,

Good to the Poore, to kindred deare,
To servants kind, to friendship cleare,
To nothing but her selfe, severe.

So though a Virgin, yet a Bride
To every Grace, she justifi'd
A chaste Poligamie, and dy'd.

Learn from hence (Reader) what small trust
We owe this world, where vertue must
Fraile as our flesh, crumble to dust.

JOHN DONNE

Holy Sonnet X

Batter my heart, three person'd God; for, you
As yet but knocke, breathe, shine, and seeke to mend;
That I may rise, and stand, o'erthrow mee,'and bend
Your force, to breake, blowe, burn and make me new.
I, like an usurpt towne, to'another due,
Labour to'admit you, but Oh, to no end,
Reason your viceroy in mee, mee should defend,
But is captiv'd, and proves weake or untrue,
Yet dearely'I love you, and would be lov'd faine,
But am betroth'd unto your enemie,
Divorce mee,'untie, or breake that knot againe,
Take mee to you, imprison mee, for I
Except you'enthrall mee, never shall be free,
Nor ever chast, except you ravish mee.

HENRY VAUGHAN

The Morning-Watch

O Joyes! Infinite sweetnes! with what flowres,
And shoots of glory, my soul breakes, and buds!
      All the long houres
      Of night, and Rest
      Through the still shrouds
      Of sleep, and Clouds,
   This Dew fell on my Breast;
      O how it *Blouds*,
And *Spirits* all my Earth! heark! In what Rings,
And *Hymning Circulations* the quick world
      Awakes, and sings;
      The rising winds,
      And falling springs,
      Birds, beasts, all things
   Adore him in their kinds.
      Thus all is hurl'd
In sacred *Hymnes*, and *Order*, the great *Chime*
And *Symphony* of nature. Prayer is
      The world in tune,
      A spirit-voyce,
      And vocall joyes
   Whose *Eccho* is heav'ns blisse.
      O let me climbe
When I lye down! The Pious soul by night
Is like a clouded starre, whose beames though sed

    To shed their light
    Under some Cloud
    Yet are above,
    And shine, and move
   Beyond that mistie shrowd.
    So in my Bed
That Curtain'd grave, though sleep, like ashes, hide
My lamp, and life, both shall in thee abide.

III

The Many Spiritual Conflicts

'... Sir, I pray deliver this little Book to my dear brother Farrer, and tell him, he shall find in it a picture of the many spiritual Conflicts that have past betwixt God and my Soul, before I could subject mine to the will of Jesus my Master....'
Walton's 'Life'

The Collar

I struck the board, and cry'd, No more.
        I will abroad.
        What? shall I ever sigh and pine?
My lines and life are free; free as the rode,
        Loose as the winde, as large as store.
        Shall I be still in suit?
        Have I no harvest but a thorn
        To let me bloud, and not restore
        What I have lost with cordiall fruit?
        Sure there was wine
Before my sighs did drie it: there was corn
        Before my tears did drown it.
    Is the yeare onely lost to me?
        Have I no bayes to crown it?
No flowers, no garlands gay? all blasted?
        All wasted?
Not so, my heart: but there is fruit,
        And thou hast hands.
Recover all thy sigh-blown age
On double pleasures: leave thy cold dispute
Of what is fit, and not. Forsake thy cage,
        Thy rope of sands,
Which pettie thoughts have made, and made to thee
        Good cable, to enforce and draw,
        And be thy law,
    While thou didst wink and wouldst not see.
        Away; take heed:
        I will abroad.

Call in thy deaths head there: tie up thy fears.
He that forbears
To suit and serve his need,
Deserves his load.
But as I rav'd and grew more fierce and wilde
At every word,
Me thoughts I heard one calling, *Child!*
And I reply'd, *My Lord.*

The Crosse

What is this strange and uncouth thing?
To make me sigh, and seek, and faint, and die,
Untill I had some place, where I might sing,
    And serve thee; and not onely I,
But all my wealth and familie might combine
To set thy honour up, as our designe.

And then when after much delay,
Much wrastling, many a combate, this deare end,
So much desir'd, is giv'n, to take away
    My power to serve thee; to unbend
All my abilities, my designes confound,
And lay my threatnings bleeding on the ground.

One ague dwelleth in my bones,
Another in my soul (the memorie
What I would do for thee, if once my grones
    Could be allow'd for harmonie):
I am in all a weak disabled thing,
Save in the sight thereof, where strength doth sting.

Besides, things sort not to my will,
Ev'n when my will doth studie thy renown:
Thou turnest th'edge of all things on me still,
    Taking me up to throw me down:
So that, ev'n when my hopes seem to be sped,
I am to grief alive, to them as dead.

   To have my aim, and yet to be
Further from it then when I bent my bow;
To make my hopes my torture, and the fee
   Of all my woes another wo,
Is in the midst of delicates to need,
And ev'n in Paradise to be a weed.

   Ah my deare Father, ease my smart!
These contrarieties crush me: these crosse actions
Doe winde a rope about, and cut my heart:
   And yet since these thy contradictions
Are properly a crosse felt by thy Sonne,
With but foure words, my words, *Thy will be done.*

Confession

O what a cunning guest
Is this same grief! within my heart I made
Closets; and in them many a chest;
And, like a master in my trade,
In those chests, boxes; in each box, a till:
Yet grief knows all, and enters when he will.

No scrue, no piercer can
Into a piece of timber work and winde,
As God's afflictions into man,
When he a torture hath design'd.
They are too subtill for the subt'llest hearts;
And fall, like rheumes, upon the tendrest parts.

We are the earth; and they,
Like moles within us, heave, and cast about:
And till they foot and clutch their prey,
They never cool, much lesse give out.
No smith can make such locks but they have keyes:
Closets are halls to them; and hearts, high-wayes.

Onely an open breast
Doth shut them out, so that they cannot enter;
Or, if they enter, cannot rest,
But quickly seek some new adventure.
Smooth open hearts no fastning have; but fiction
Doth give a hold and handle to affliction.

Wherefore my faults and sinnes,
Lord, I acknowledge; take thy plagues away:
For since confession pardon winnes,
I challenge here the brightest day,
The clearest diamond: let them do their best,
They shall be thick and cloudie to my breast.

Conscience

    Peace pratler, do not lowre:
Not a fair look, but thou dost call it foul:
Not a sweet dish, but thou dost call it sowre:
      Musick to thee doth howl.
   By listing to thy chatting fears
   I have lost both mine eyes and eares.

    Pratler, no more, I say:
My thoughts must work, but like a noiselesse sphere;
Harmonious peace must rock them all the day:
      No room for pratlers there.
   If thou persistest, I will tell thee,
   That I have physick to expell thee.

    And the receit shall be
My Saviours bloud: when ever at his board
I do but taste it, straight it cleanseth me,
      And leaves thee not a word;
   No, not a tooth or nail to scratch,
   And at my actions carp, or catch.

    Yet if thou talkest still,
Besides my physick, know there's some for thee:
Some wood and nails to make a staffe or bill
      For those that trouble me:
   The bloudie crosse of my deare Lord
   Is both my physick and my sword.

Affliction (I)

When first thou didst entice to thee my heart,
              I thought the service brave:
So many joyes I writ down for my part,
              Besides what I might have
Out of my stock of naturall delights,
Augmented with thy gracious benefits.

I looked on thy furniture so fine,
              And made it fine to me:
Thy glorious household-stuffe did me entwine,
              And 'tice me unto thee.
Such starres I counted mine: both heav'n and earth
Payd me my wages in a world of mirth.

What pleasures could I want, whose King I served,
              Where joyes my fellows were?
Thus argu'd into hopes, my thoughts reserved
              No place for grief or fear.
Therefore my sudden soul caught at the place,
And made her youth and fierceness seek thy face.

At first thou gav'st me milk and sweetnesses;
              I had my wish and way:
My dayes were straw'd with flow'rs and happinesse;
              There was no moneth but May.
But with my yeares sorrow did twist and grow,
And made a partie unawares for wo.

My flesh began unto my soul in pain,
>> Sicknesses cleave my bones;
Consuming agues dwell in ev'ry vein,
>> And tune my breath to grones.
Sorrow was all my soul; I scarce beleeved,
Till grief did tell me roundly, that I lived.

When I got health, thou took'st away my life,
>> And more; for my friends die:
My mirth and edge was lost; a blunted knife
>> Was of more use then I.
Thus thinne and lean without a fence or friend,
I was blown through with ev'ry storm and winde.

Whereas my birth and spirit rather took
>> The way that takes the town;
Thou didst betray me to a lingring book,
>> And wrap me in a gown.
I was entangled in the world of strife,
Before I had the power to change my life.

Yet, for I threatned oft the siege to raise,
>> Not simpring all mine age,
Thou often didst with Academick praise
>> Melt and dissolve my rage.
I took thy sweetned pill, till I came where
I could not go away, nor persevere.

Yet lest perchance I should too happie be
>> In my unhappinesse,
Turning my purge to food, thou throwest me
>> Into more sicknesses.
Thus doth thy power crosse-bias me, not making
Thine own gift good, yet me from my wayes taking.

Now I am here, what thou wilt do with me
                None of my books will show:
I reade, and sigh, and wish I were a tree;
                For sure then I should grow
To fruit or shade: at least some bird would trust
Her household to me, and I should be just.

Yet, though thou troublest me, I must be meek;
                In weakness must be stout.
Well, I will change the service, and go seek
                Some other master out.
Ah my deare God! though I am clean forgot,
Let me not love thee, if I love thee not.

Affliction (IV)

Broken in pieces all asunder
        Lord, hunt me not,
        A thing forgot,
Once a poore creature, now a wonder,
        A wonder tortur'd in the space
        Betwixt this world and that of grace.

My thoughts are all a case of knives,
        Wounding my heart
        With scatter'd smart,
As watring pots give flowers their lives.
        Nothing their furie can controll
        While they do wound and pink my soul.

All my attendants are at strife,
        Quitting their place
        Unto my face:
Nothing performs the task of life:
        The elements are let loose to fight,
        And while I live, trie out their right.

Oh help, my God! let not their plot
        Kill them and me,
        And also thee,
Who are my life: dissolve the knot,
        As the sunne scatters by his light
        All the rebellions of the night.

Then shall those powers, which work for grief,
>   Enter thy pay,
>   And day by day
Labour thy praise, and my relief;
>   With care and courage building me,
>   Till I reach heav'n, and much more, thee.

The Pearl

I know the wayes of Learning; both the head
And pipes that feed the presse, and make it runne;
What reason hath from nature borrowed,
Or of it self, like a good huswife, spunne
In laws and policie; what the starres conspire,
What willing nature speaks, what forc'd by fire;
Both th'old discoveries, and the new-found seas,
The stock and surplus, cause and historie:
All these stand open, or I have the keyes:
      Yet I love thee.

I know the wayes of Honour, what maintains
The quick returns of courtesie and wit:
In vies of favours whether partie gains,
When glorie swells the heart, and moldeth it
To all expressions both of hand and eye,
Which on the world a true-love-knot may tie,
And bear the bundle, wheresoe're it goes:
How many drammes of spirit there must be
To sell my life unto my friends or foes:
      Yet I love thee.

I know the wayes of Pleasure, the sweet strains,
The lullings and the relishes of it;
The propositions of hot bloud and brains;
What mirth and musick mean; what love and wit
Have done these twentie hundred yeares, and more:
I know the projects of unbridled store:
My stuffe is flesh, not brasse; my senses live,
And grumble oft, that they have more in me
Than he that curbs them, being but one to five:
      Yet I love thee.

I know all these, and have them in my hand:
Therefore not sealed, but with open eyes
I flie to thee, and fully understand
Both the main sale, and the commodities;
And at what rate and price I have thy love;
With all the circumstances that may move:
Yet through these labyrinths, not my groveling wit,
But thy silk twist let down from heav'n to me,
Did both conduct and teach me, how by it
          To climbe to thee.

The Flower

How fresh, O Lord, how sweet and clean
Are thy returns! ev'n as the flowers in spring;
To which, besides their own demean,
The late-past frosts tributes of pleasure bring.
         Grief melts away
         Like snow in May,
As if there were no such cold thing.

Who would have thought my shrivel'd heart
Could have recover'd greennesse? It was gone
      Quite under ground; as flowers depart
To see their mother-root, when they have blown;
         Where they together
         All the hard weather,
Dead to the world, keep house unknown.

These are thy wonders, Lord of power,
Killing and quickning, bringing down to hell
      And up to heaven in an houre;
Making a chiming of a passing-bell.
         We say amisse,
         This or that is:
Thy word is all, if we could spell.

O that I once past changing were,
Fast in thy Paradise, where no flower can wither!
      Many a spring I shoot up fair,
Off'ring at heav'n, growing and groning thither:
         Nor doth my flower
         Want a spring-showre,
My sinnes and I joining together.

But while I grow in a straight line,
Still upwards bent, as if heav'n were mine own,
   Thy anger comes, and I decline:
What frost to that? what pole is not the zone,
        Where all things burn,
        When thou dost turn,
   And the least frown of thine is shown?

And now in age I bud again,
After so many deaths I live and write;
   I once more smell the dew and rain,
And relish versing: O my onely light,
        It cannot be
        That I am he
   On whom thy tempests fell all night.

These are thy wonders, Lord of love,
To make us see we are but flowers that glide:
   Which when we once can finde and prove,
Thou hast a garden for us, where to bide.
        Who would be more,
        Swelling through store,
   Forfeit their Paradise by their pride.

The Pilgrimage

I travell'd on, seeing the hill, where lay
          My expectation.
    A long it was and weary way.
    The gloomy cave of Desperation
I left on th'one, and on the other side
          The rock of Pride.

And so I came to Fancies medow strow'd
          With many a flower:
    Fain would I here have made abode,
    But I was quicken'd by my houre.
So to Cares cops I came, and there got through
          With much ado.

That led me to the wilde of Passion, which
          Some call the wold;
    A wasted place, but sometimes rich.
    Here I was robb'd of all my gold,
Save one good Angell, which a friend had ti'd
          Close to my side.

At length I got unto the gladsome hill,
          Where lay my hope,
    Where lay my heart; and climbing still,
    When I had gain'd the brow and top,
A lake of brackish waters on the ground
          Was all I found.

With that abash'd and struck with many a sting
           Of swarming fears,
    I fell, and cry'd, Alas my King!
      Can both the way and end be tears?
Yet taking heart I rose, and then perceiv'd
           I was deceiv'd:

My hill was further: so I flung away,
           Yet heard a crie
    Just as I went, *None goes that way*
      And lives: If that be all, said I,
After so foul a journey death is fair,
           And but a chair.

JOHN DONNE

A Hymne to God the Father

Wilt thou forgive that sinne where I begunne,
   Which is my sin, though it were done before?
Wilt thou forgive those sinnes through which I runne,
   And doe them still: though still I doe deplore?
     When thou hast done, thou hast not done,
        For, I have more.

Wilt thou forgive that sinne by which I wonne
   Others to sinne? and, made my sinne their doore?
Wilt thou forgive that sinne which I did shunne
   A yeare, or two: but wallowed in, a score?
     When thou hast done, thou hast not done,
        For, I have more.

I have a sinne of feare, that when I have spunne
   My last thred, I shall perish on the shore;
Sweare by thy selfe, that at my death thy Sunne
   Shall shine as it shines now, and heretofore;
     And, having done that, Thou hast done,
        I have no more.

ANDREW MARVELL

A Dialogue between the Soul and Body

Soul   O who shall, from this Dungeon, raise
A Soul inslav'd so many wayes?
With bolts of Bones, that fetter'd stands
In Feet; and manacled in Hands.
Here blinded with an Eye; and there
Deaf with the drumming of an Ear.
A Soul hung up, as 'twere, in Chains
Of Nerves, and Arteries, and Veins.
Tortur'd, besides each other part,
In a vain Head, and double Heart.

Body   Oh who shall me deliver whole,
From bonds of this Tyrannic Soul?
Which, stretcht upright, impales me so,
That mine own Precipice I go;
And warms and moves this needless Frame:
(A Fever could but do the same.)
And, wanting where its spight to try,
Has made me live to let me dye.
A Body that could never rest,
Since this ill Spirit it possest.

Soul   What Magick could me thus confine
Within anothers Grief to pine?
Where whatsoever it complain,
I feel, that cannot feel, the pain.

        And all my Care its self employes,
        That to preserve, which me destroys:
        Constrain'd not only to indure
        Diseases, but, whats worse, the Cure:
        And ready oft the Port to gain,
        Am Shipwrackt into Health again.

Body   But Physick yet could never reach
        The Maladies Thou me dost teach;
        Whom first the Cramp of Hope does Tear:
        And then the Palsie Shakes of Fear.
        The Pestilence of Love does heat:
        Or Hatred's hidden Ulcer eat.
        Joy's chearful Madness does perplex:
        Or Sorrow's other Madness vex.
        Which Knowledge forces me to know;
        And Memory will not foregoe.
        What but a Soul could have the wit
        To build me up for Sin so fit?
        So Architects do square and hew
        Green Trees that in the Forest grew.

IV

Poetry of Meditation

'... Meditation which we treate of, is nothing els but a diligent and forcible application of the understanding, to seeke, and knowe, and as it were to tast some divine matter....'

Bruno's 'Meditations'

Aaron

Holinesse on the head,
Light and perfections on the breast,
Harmonious bells below, raising the dead
To leade them unto life and rest:
    Thus are true Aarons drest.

Profaneness in my head
Defects and darknesse in my breast,
A noise of passions ringing me for dead
Unto a place where is no rest:
    Poore priest thus am I drest.

Onely another head
I have, another heart and breast,
Another musick, making live not dead,
Without whom I could have no rest:
    In him I am well drest.

Christ is my onely head,
My alone onely heart and breast,
My onely musick, striking me ev'n dead;
That to the old man I may rest,
    And be in him new drest.

So holy in my head,
Perfect and light in my deare breast,
My doctrine tun'd by Christ (who is not dead
But lives in me while I do rest)
    Come people; Aaron's drest.

The Pulley

When God at first made man,
Having a glasse of blessings standing by;
Let us (said he) poure on him all we can:
Let the worlds riches, which dispersed lie,
    Contract into a span.

So strength first made a way;
Then beautie flow'd, then wisdome, honour, pleasure:
When almost all was out, God made a stay,
Perceiving that alone of all his treasure
    Rest in the bottome lay.

For if I should (said he)
Bestow this jewell also on my creature,
He would adore my gifts in stead of me,
And rest in Nature, not the God of Nature:
    So both should losers be.

Yet let him keep the rest,
But keep them with repining restlesnesse:
Let him be rich and wearie, that at least,
If goodnesse leade him not, yet wearinesse
    May tosse him to my breast.

Prayer (II)

Of what an easie quick accesse
My blessed Lord, art thou! how suddenly
    May our requests thine eare invade!
To shew that state dislikes not easinesse,
If I but lift mine eyes, my suit is made:
Thou canst no more not heare, then thou canst die.

    Of what supreme almightie power
Is thy great arm, which spans the east and west,
    And tacks the centre to the sphere!
By it do all things live their measur'd houre:
We cannot ask the thing, which is not there,
Blaming the shallownesse of our request.

    Of what unmeasurable love
Art thou possest, who, when thou couldst not die,
    Wert fain to take our flesh and curse,
And for our sakes in person sinne reprove,
That by destroying that which ty'd thy purse,
Thou mightst make way for liberalitie!

    Since then these three wait on thy throne,
Ease, *Power*, and *Love*; I value prayer so,
    That were I to leave all but one,
Wealth, fame, endowments, vertues, all should go;
I and deare prayer would together dwell,
And quickly gain, for each inch lost, an ell.

The Agonie

    Philosophers have measur'd mountains,
Fathom'd the depths of seas, of states, and kings,
Walk'd with a staffe to heav'n, and traced fountains:
    But there are two vast, spacious things,
The which to measure it doth more behove:
Yet few there are that sound them; Sinne and Love.

    Who would know Sinne, let him repair
Unto Mount Olivet; there shall he see
A man so wrung with pains, that all his hair,
    His skinne, his garments bloudie be.
Sinne is that presse and vice, which forceth pain
To hunt his cruell food through ev'ry vein.

    Who knows not Love, let him assay
And taste that juice, which on the crosse a pike
Did set again abroach; then let him say
    If ever he did taste the like.
Love is that liquor sweet and most divine,
Which my God feels as bloud; but I, as wine.

The Sacrifice

Oh all ye, who passe by, whose eyes and minde
To wordly things are sharp, but to me blinde;
To me, who took eyes that I might you finde:
        Was ever grief like mine?

The Princes of my people make a head
Against their Maker: they do wish me dead,
Who cannot wish, except I give them bread:
        Was ever grief like mine?

Without me each one, who doth now me brave,
Had to this day been an Egyptian slave.
They use that power against me, which I gave:
        Was ever grief like mine?

Mine own Apostle, who the bag did beare,
Though he had all I had, did not forbeare
To sell me also, and to put me there:
        Was ever grief like mine?

For thirtie pence he did my death devise,
Who at three hundred did the ointment prize,
Not half so sweet as my sweet sacrifice:
        Was ever grief like mine?

Therefore my soul melts, and my hearts deare treasure
Drops bloud (the onely beads) my words to measure:
O let this cup passe, if it be thy pleasure:
        Was ever grief like mine?

These drops being temper'd with a sinners tears
A Balsome are for both the Hemispheres:
Curing all wounds, but mine; all, but my fears:
   Was ever grief like mine?

Yet my Disciples sleep: I cannot gain
One houre of watching; but their drowsie brain
Comforts not me, and doth my doctrine stain:
   Was ever grief like mine?

Arise, arise, they come. Look how they runne!
Alas! what haste they make to be undone!
How with their lanterns do they seek the sunne!
   Was ever grief like mine?

With clubs and staves they seek me, as a thief,
Who am the Way and Truth, the true relief;
Most true to those, who are my greatest grief:
   Was ever grief like mine?

Judas, dost thou betray me with a kisse?
Canst thou finde hell about my lips? and misse
Of life, just at the gates of life and blisse?
   Was ever grief like mine?

See, they lay hold on me, not with the hands
Of faith, but furie: yet at their commands
I suffer binding, who have loos'd their bands:
   Was ever grief like mine?

All my Disciples flie; fear puts a barre
Betwixt my friends and me. They leave the starre,
That brought the wise men of the East from farre.
   Was ever grief like mine?

Then from one ruler to another bound
They leade me; urging, that it was not sound
What I taught: Comments would the text confound.
           Was ever grief like mine?

The Priest and rulers all false witnesse seek
'Gainst him, who seeks not life, but is the meek
And readie Paschal Lambe of this great week:
           Was ever grief like mine?

Then they accuse me of great blasphemie,
That I did thrust into the Deitie,
Who never thought that any robberie:
           Was ever grief like mine?

Some said, that I the Temple to the floore
In three dayes raz'd, and raised as before.
Why, he that built the world can do much more:
           Was ever grief like mine?

Then they condemne me all with that same breath,
Which I do give them daily, unto death.
Thus *Adam* my first breathing rendereth:
           Was ever grief like mine?

They binde, and leade me unto *Herod*: he
Sends me to *Pilate*. This makes them agree;
But yet their friendship is my enmitie:
           Was ever grief like mine?

Herod and all his bands do set me light,
Who teach all hands to warre, fingers to fight,
And onely am the Lord of Hosts and might:
           Was ever grief like mine?

Herod in judgement sits, while I do stand;
Examines me with a censorious hand:
I him obey, who all things else command:
                Was ever grief like mine?

The *Jews* accuse me with despitefulnesse;
And vying malice with my gentlenesse,
Pick quarrels with their onely happinesse:
                Was ever grief like mine?

I answer nothing, but with patience prove
If stonie hearts will melt with gentle love.
But who does hawk at eagles with a dove?
                Was ever grief like mine?

My silence rather doth augment their crie;
My dove doth back into my bosome flie,
Because the raging waters still are high:
                Was ever grief like mine?

Heark how they crie aloud still, *Crucifie:*
It is not fit he live a day, they crie,
Who cannot live lesse than eternally:
                Was ever grief like mine?

Pilate, a stranger, holdeth off; but they,
Mine owne deare people, cry, *Away, away*,
With noises confused frighting the day:
                Was ever grief like mine?

Yet still they shout, and crie, and stop their eares,
Putting my life among their sinnes and feares,
And therefore wish *my bloud on them and theirs*:
                Was ever grief like mine?

See how spite cankers things. These words aright
Used, and wished, are the whole worlds light:
But hony is their gall, brightnesse their night:
    Was ever grief like mine?

They choose a murderer, and all agree
In him to do themselves a courtesie:
For it was their own case who killed me:
    Was ever grief like mine?

And a seditious murderer he was:
But I the Prince of peace; peace that doth passe
All understanding, more than heav'n doth glasse:
    Was ever grief like mine?

Why, Caesar is their onely King, not I:
He clave the stonie rock, when they were drie;
But surely not their hearts, as I well trie:
    Was ever grief like mine?

Ah! how they scourge me! yet my tendernesse
Doubles each lash: and yet their bitternesse
Windes up my grief to a mysteriousnesse:
    Was ever grief like mine?

They buffet him, and box him as they list,
Who grasps the earth and heaven with his fist,
And never yet, whom he would punish, miss'd:
    Was ever grief like mine?

Behold, they spit on me in scornfull wise,
Who by my spittle gave the blinde man eies,
Leaving his blindnesse to my enemies:
    Was ever grief like mine?

My face they cover, though it be divine.
As *Moses* face was vailed, so is mine,
Lest on their double-dark souls either shine:
                Was ever grief like mine?

Servants and abjects flout me; they are wittie:
Now prophesie who strikes thee, is their dittie.
So they in me denie themselves all pitie:
                Was ever grief like mine?

And now am I deliver'd unto death,
Which each one calls for so with utmost breath,
That he before me well nigh suffereth:
                Was ever grief like mine?

Weep not, deare friends, since I for both have wept
When all my tears were bloud, the while you slept:
Your tears for your own fortunes should be kept:
                Was ever grief like mine?

The souldiers lead me to the Common Hall;
There they deride me, they abuse me all:
Yet for twelve heav'nly legions I could call:
                Was ever grief like mine?

Then with a scarlet robe they me array;
Which shews my bloud to be the onely way
And cordiall left to repair mans decay:
                Was ever grief like mine?

Then on my head a crown of thorns I wear:
For these are all the grapes Sion doth bear,
Though I my vine planted and watred there:
                Was ever grief like mine?

So sits the earths great curse in *Adams* fall
Upon my head: so I remove it all
From th'earth unto my brows, and bear the thrall:
            Was ever grief like mine?

Then with the reed they gave to me before,
They strike my head, the rock from whence all store
Of heav'nly blessings issue evermore:
            Was ever grief like mine?

They bow their knees to me, and cry, *Hail King*:
What ever scoffes & scornfulnesse can bring,
I am the floore, the sink, where they it fling:
            Was ever grief like mine?

Yet since mans scepters are as frail as reeds,
And thorny all their crowns, bloudie their weeds;
I, who am Truth, turn into truth their deeds:
            Was ever grief like mine?

The souldiers also spit upon that face,
Which Angels did desire to have the grace,
And Prophets, once to see, but found no place:
            Was ever grief like mine?

Thus trimmed, forth they bring me to the rout,
Who *Crucifie him*, crie with one strong shout.
God holds his peace at man, and man cries out:
            Was ever grief like mine?

They leade me in once more, and putting then
Mine own clothes on, they leade me out agen.
Whom devils flie, thus is he toss'd of men:
            Was ever grief like mine?

And now wearie of sport, glad to ingrosse
All spite in one, counting my life their losse,
They carrie me to my most bitter crosse:
                Was ever grief like mine?

My crosse I bear my self, untill I faint:
Then Simon bears it for me by constraint,
The decreed burden of each mortall Saint:
                Was ever grief like mine?

O all ye who passe by, behold and see;
Man stole the fruit, but I must climbe the tree;
The tree of life to all, but onely me:
                Was ever grief like mine?

Lo, here I hang, charg'd with a world of sinne,
The greater world o'th'two; for that came in
By words, but this by sorrow I must win:
                Was ever grief like mine?

Such sorrow as, if sinfull man could feel,
Or feel his part, he would not cease to kneel,
Till all were melted, though he were all steel:
                Was ever grief like mine?

But, *O my God, my God!* why leav'st thou me,
The sonne, in whom thou dost delight to be?
My God, my God——
                Never was grief like mine.

Shame tears my soul, my bodie many a wound;
Sharp nails pierce this, but sharper that confound;
Reproches, which are free, while I am bound.
                Was ever grief like mine?

Now heal thy self, Physician; now come down.
Alas! I did so, when I left my crown
And fathers smile for you, to feel his frown:
>   Was ever grief like mine?

In healing not my self, there doth consist
All that salvation, which ye now resist;
Your safetie in my sicknesse doth subsist:
>   Was ever grief like mine?

Betwixt two theeves I spend my utmost breath,
As he that for some robberie suffereth.
Alas! what have I stollen from you? Death.
>   Was ever grief like mine?

A king my title is, prefixt on high;
Yet by my subjects am condemn'd to die
A servile death in servile companie:
>   Was ever grief like mine?

They give me vinegar mingled with gall,
But more with malice: yet, when they did call,
With Manna, Angels food, I fed them all:
>   Was ever grief like mine?

They part my garments, and by lot dispose
My coat, the type of love, which once cur'd those
Who sought for help, never malicious foes:
>   Was ever grief like mine?

Nay, after death their spite shall further go;
For they will pierce my side, I full well know;
That as sinne came, so Sacraments might flow:
>   Was ever grief like mine?

But now I die; now all is finished.
My wo, mans weal: and now I bow my head.
Onely let others say, when I am dead,
                  Never was grief like mine.

HENRY KING

The Exequy

To his Matchlesse never to be forgotten Freind

Accept thou Shrine of my dead Saint,
Insteed of Dirges this complaint;
And for sweet flowres to crown thy hearse,
Receive a strew of weeping verse
From thy griev'd friend, whom thou might'st see
Quite melted into tears for thee.

    Dear loss! since thy untimely fate
My task hath been to meditate
On thee, on thee: thou art the book,
The library whereon I look
Though almost blind. For thee (lov'd clay)
I languish out, not live the day,
Using no other exercise
But what I practise with mine eyes:
By which wet glasses I find out
How lazily time creeps about
To one that mourns: this, onely this
My exercise and bus'ness is:
So I compute the weary houres
With sighs dissolved into showres.

    Nor wonder if my time go thus
Backward and most preposterous;
Thou hast benighted me, thy set

This Eve of blackness did beget,
Who was't my day (though overcast)
Before thou had'st thy Noon-tide past
And I remember must in tears,
Thou scarce had'st seen so many years
As Day tells houres. By thy cleer Sun
My life and fortunes first did run;
But thou wilt never more appear
Folded within my Hemisphere.
Since both thy light and motion
Like a fled Star is fall'n and gon,
And twixt me and my soules dear wish
The earth now interposed is,
Which such a strange eclipse doth make
As ne're was read in Almanake.
I could allow thee for a time
To darken me and my sad Clime,
Were it a month, a year, or ten,
I would thy exile live till then;
And all that space my mirth adjourn,
So thou wouldst promise to return;
And putting off thy ashy shrowd
At length disperse this sorrows cloud.

    But woe is me! the longest date
Too narrow is to calculate
These empty hopes: never shall I
Be so much blest as to descry
A glimpse of thee, till that day come
Which shall the earth to cinders doome,
And a fierce Feaver must calcine
The body of this world like thine,
(My little World!). That fit of fire
Once off, our bodies shall aspire
To our soules bliss: then we shall rise
And view our selves with cleerer eyes

In that calm Region, where no night
Can hide us from each others sight.

    Mean time, thou hast her, earth: much good
May my harm do thee. Since it stood
With Heavens will I might not call
Her longer mine, I give thee all
My short-liv'd right and interest
In her, whom living I lov'd best:
With a most free and bounteous grief,
I give thee what I could not keep.
Be kind to her, and prethee look
Thou write into thy Dooms-day book
Each parcell of this Rarity
Which in thy Casket shrin'd doth ly:
See that thou make thy reck'ning streight,
And yield her back again by weight;
For thou must audit on thy trust
Each graine and atome of this dust,
As thou wilt answer *Him* that lent,
Not gave thee, my dear Monument.

    So close the ground, and 'bout her shade
Black curtains draw, my *Bride* is laid.

    Sleep on my *Love* in thy cold bed
Never to be disquieted!
My last good night! Thou wilt not wake
Till I thy fate shall overtake:
Till age, or grief, or sickness must
Marry my body to that dust
It so much loves; and fill the room
My heart keeps empty in thy Tomb.
Stay for me there; I will not faile
To meet thee in that hollow Vale.
And think not much of my delay;

I am already on the way,
And follow thee with all the speed
Desire can make, or sorrows breed.
Each minute is a short degree,
And ev'ry houre a step towards thee.
At night when I betake to rest,
Next morn I rise neerer my West
Of life, almost by eight houres saile,
Than when sleep breath'd his drowsie gale.

    Thus from the Sun my Bottom stears,
And my dayes Compass downward bears:
Nor labour I to stemme the tide
Through which to *Thee* I swiftly glide.

    Tis true, with shame and grief I yield,
Thou like the *Vann* first took'st the field,
And gotten hast the victory
In thus adventuring to dy
Before me, whose more years might crave
A just precedence in the grave.
But heark! My pulse like a soft Drum
Beats my approach, tells *Thee* I come;
And slow howere my marches be,
I shall at last sit down by *Thee*.

    The thought of this bids me go on,
And wait my dissolution
With hope and comfort. *Dear* (forgive
The crime) I am content to live
Divided, with but half a heart,
Till we shall meet and never part.

JOHN DONNE

Goodfriday, 1613: Riding Westward

Let mans Soule be a Spheare, and then, in this,
The intelligence that moves, devotion is,
And as the other Spheares, by being growne
Subject to forraigne motions, lose their owne,
And being by others hurried every day,
Scarce in a yeare their naturall forme obey:
Pleasure or businesse, so, our Soules admit
For their first mover, and are whirld by it.
Hence is't, that I am carryed towards the West
This day, when my Soules forme bends toward the East.
There I should see a Sunne, by rising set,
And by that setting endlesse day beget;
But that Christ on this Crosse, did rise and fall,
Sinne had eternally benighted all.
Yet dare I'almost be glad, I do not see
That spectacle of too much weight for mee.
Who sees Gods face, that is selfe life, must dye;
What a death were it then to see God dye?
It made his owne Lieutenant Nature shrinke,
It made his footstoole crack, and the Sunne winke.
Could I behold those hands which span the Poles,
And tune all spheares at once, peirc'd with those holes?
Could I behold that endlesse height which is
Zenith to us, and to'our Antipodes,
Humbled below us? or that blood which is
The seat of all our Soules, if not of his,
Make durt of dust, or that flesh which was worne

By God, for his apparell, rag'd, and torne?
If on these things I durst not looke, durst I
Upon his miserable mother cast mine eye,
Who was Gods partner here, and furnish'd thus
Halfe of that Sacrifice, which ransom'd us?
Though these things, as I ride, be from mine eye,
They'are present yet unto my memory.
For that looks towards them; and thou look'st towards mee,
O Saviour, as thou hang'st upon the tree;
I turne my backe to thee, but to receive
Corrections, till thy mercies bid thee leave.
O thinke mee worth thine anger, punish mee,
Burne off my rusts, and my deformity,
Restore thine Image, so much, by thy grace,
That thou may'st know mee, and I'll turne my face.

ANDREW MARVELL

To his Coy Mistress

Had we but World enough, and Time,
This coyness Lady were no crime.
We would sit down, and think which way
To walk, and pass our long Loves Day.
Thou by the *Indian Ganges* side
Should'st rubies find: I by the Tide
Of *Humber* would complain. I would
Love you ten years before the Flood:
And you should if you please refuse
Till the Conversion of the *Jews*.
My vegetable Love should grow
Vaster than Empires, and more slow.
An hundred years should go to praise
Thine Eyes, and on thy Forehead Gaze.
Two hundred to adore each Breast:
But thirty thousand to the rest.
An Age at least to every part,
And the last Age should show your Heart.
For Lady you deserve this State;
Nor would I love at lower rate.

But at my back I alwaies hear
Times winged Charriot hurrying near:
And yonder all before us lye
Desarts of vast Eternity.
Thy Beauty shall no more be found;
Nor, in thy marble Vault, shall sound

My ecchoing Song: then Worms shall try
That long preserv'd Virginity:
And your quaint Honour turn to dust;
And into ashes all my Lust.
The Grave's a fine and private place,
But none I think do there embrace.

 Now therefore, while the youthful hew
Sits on thy skin like morning dew,
And while thy willing Soul transpires
At every pore with instant Fires,
Now let us sport us while we may;
And now, like am'rous birds of prey,
Rather at once our Time devour
Than languish in his slow-chapt pow'r.
Let us roll all our Strength, and all
Our sweetness, up into one Ball:
And tear our Pleasures with rough strife,
Thorough the Iron gates of Life.
Thus, though we cannot make our Sun
Stand still, yet we will make him run.

Critical Commentary and Notes

I   HYMNS AND ANTHEMS

   Commentary   103–107
   Notes   108–112

II HIS QUICK-PIERCING MIND

   Commentary   113–118
   Notes   118–124

III THE MANY SPIRITUAL CONFLICTS

   Commentary   125–131
   Notes   132–139

IV POETRY OF MEDITATION

   Commentary   140–145
   Notes   145–150

I Hymns and Anthems

It seems well to begin with some poems that are probably familiar to many readers: poems still in use as hymns, songs whose simplicity and directness are real. They were composed for music, and obey the needs of music—firm, dependable metres, each stanza a replica of the others, refrains, and so on. *Vertue* is the only one of this group not definitely for music, but it perfectly exemplifies the effect of Herbert's feeling for music and the disciplines of song, whether it was ever sung or not. Simplicity, neatness, directness, candour—these are the first-apparent qualities. But they give us less than the whole truth. The very familiarity of one or two of these poems may have set scales to our eyes which the chance to read them carefully and sensitively can remove. However he aspires to simplicity, Herbert cannot, and will not, altogether restrain his habitual delicacy and acumen; his are perhaps the most *pointed* hymns to be found in our hymn-books. It will be an unusual group reading these poems together that contains even one reader who can claim to have engaged all the points of the famous *Elixir*. To begin with, he or she will need to have been attentive enough to realize that the versions usually sung have something missing; have an awkward hiatus in the development of the theme: and to have looked up the original to discover verse 2. There is no better way to come at Herbert's quality than this realizing how much more he demands, and how much more he has to offer, than the majority of hymn-writers.

Praise, for instance, requires a sharper attention than we are used to giving the hymns we sing in Church, or at an assembly:

> Wherefore with my utmost art
> I will sing thee,
> And the cream of all my heart
> I will bring thee.

This third verse reminds us that the simplicity of such song, its dignified sincerity, represent for Herbert an achievement of 'utmost art'. It has not come easily. And that art is not a matter of superficial expertise, for Herbert by rhyme and by stress joins the word 'heart' to it. His utmost art in verse is to cream off the richness of his heart's feeling and offer that to God. The image is homely and practical and quite without false pride or reservation; it tastes upon the tongue, it belongs in the kitchen and the dairy.

How, then, does this 'utmost art' show itself here? First, in the candour and unaffected dignity everyone notices. That does not come easily or unsought, as any will know who have tried to get an equal dignity and sincerity into a poem or prayer of their own. There is a complete, unfeigned self-giving in praise like this that is costly to the spirit, and still requires hard exercise of skill. Then observe the verses of the song as a sequence. They alternate: a verse to God and a verse to myself. The verses for 'thee' are quick with impulsive delight like the one quoted, or like

> Sev'n whole dayes, not one in seven,
> I will praise thee.
> In my heart, though not in heaven,
> I can raise thee.

But as soon as we take our attention from the alternating sequence and fasten upon one of its verses, something else strikes home. The second of those couplets is not easily to be exhausted. There is always room, the words say, for God to be lifted higher in the heart's esteem, for He is never high enough; He is never so high as He ought to be; never so high but it lies within the heart's real capacity to set Him higher ('I *can* raise thee'). Then the qualifying clause 'though not in heaven' enriches the meaning further.

He is unimaginably beyond any adequate praising by any human heart, 'high as the heavens are from the earth'. When we meditate those two thoughts together, the couplet suggests a third meaning, deeper, and arising from the conjunction. The heart that raises up its Lord is conscious how far from being itself 'in heaven' it is, by the very need of so exerting itself to raise Him.

Now this is not so much complicated thinking as rich thinking: thinking a sudden accumulation of thoughts, deeply connected with each other; and thinking them in one glad, economical utterance. We get a sense of pressure upon the words and upon the syntax. Herbert does not use our language in an enigmatic or astonishing fashion, but he makes ordinary, unobtrusive speech work very hard, he senses and controls extraordinary suggestions in it.

Leaving aside for the moment the penultimate verse, which follows a pattern of its own, the next God-centred verse is the last of the poem. Given the clue that 'extoll' has properly the meaning 'lift up' as well as its current 'give honour to' it will be worth working out some of the ways in which that final verse really is final and draws into itself those pairs of verbs that have successively dominated each alternate verse, the first, the third and the fifth. But once we have those verbs before us, we shall also have our senses sharpened for Herbert's subtle and pointed use of syntax itself. He has made a metrical shape for his poem that brings each pair of lines to culminate in a verb, an active verb, with 'thee', or 'me', as its object. Little wonder that the praise throughout feels like a real activity, not a routine devotion. Those verbs take the weight as the voice naturally speaks the couplet; they share with 'thee' and 'me' the musical weight of the rhyming; and any trained musician of Herbert's time, setting the lines, would have followed the instinctive impetus and rhythm of the voice in his melodic line and the phrasing of it. (Having noted, now, the musical weight attaching to the rhymes of those verbs and objects, this would be a good moment at which to pause and enquire just what Herbert gains in the joining together of each rhyming word throughout—as, earlier, we noticed the point of joining 'art' with 'heart'.)

Very possibly, though, bent upon this new attention, and starting with the first verse, we shall be held up by something else:

> King of Glorie, King of Peace,
> > I will love thee:
> And that love may never cease,
> > I will move thee.

The second couplet there is busy, not only with 'love' and 'move' but with setting in motion the continual changing of places between 'thee' and 'me', the praised and the praiser, which offered a clue to the poem's structure. 'I will love thee' makes the loving of God the result of human willing, simply: and Herbert's alert mind is quick to notice a discrepancy. We do not so simply control our affections, least of all our capacity to love God. That will not do for valid theology, and it will not do for moral honesty either. God is the Cause, He is the First Mover; He is the creator of the heart that loves, the sustainer of that love within the heart. And so, like someone catching himself out in a rash promise to do more than he can, Herbert modifies 'I will love thee' with a prayer to the First Mover that the love may be unceasingly sustained. For there is another sense of that word in which man, in his turn, may 'move' God. Now we can see better *why* in the second verse subject and object change place—and why the changes continue from verse to verse. This is a verse about 'me', and God, therefore, is its Subject: and with what gay emphasis Herbert drives home the point—every line, not merely every other line, begins with 'Thou'. If we go on to trace out 'thou' and 'me' from verse to verse we find with every change some delicate significance.

Now that we have come to the verses about 'me' we should observe a difference in their tone and rhythm. The buoyancy and thrust have gone, and we have to find quite other terms to describe what takes their place. The perplexities that beset the self, once it, not God, is the object, make for difficulties of speech. No sooner, for instance, has 'the cream of all my heart' been named than it curdles. In the next lines the clamorous noises of sin's making drown the song of praise Herbert desires to offer. And even when God restores the penitent, it is those clamorous sins that interrupt, making answer for him, rudely shouting down the deeper, speechless gratitude of his true self. Yet this difficult verse about the thwarted self is still a praise of God. For He listens to and hears, not the clamour, but the penitence; He matches courtesy with courtesy:

> And alone, when they reply'd
> Thou didst hear me.

(That is, both 'You had ears only for me, despite the noise of their reply' and 'You heard, and you are the only one who could and did'. The placing of that word 'alone' so as to *command* both readings of the syntax is a characteristic touch.)

The poem reaches the fine point of its art, and its intensity, in the last verse but one. What, we have to ask, has dropped out, here, as we look back over the pattern of the whole so far? And then, why does this omission enable the final verse to sound so secure at last? And then, what ought we to make of the rhyming words that end each couplet of this verse? These are the kind of questions to pursue—and this more malicious one, too: why do the hymn-books choose this verse for omission?

Praise (albeit damagingly cut) is one of the 'familiar' Herbert poems, one of the hymns we may have sung often as if it made no real demands on our intelligence or our honesty in appraising ourselves. It is not more demanding, however, than the famous *Elixir*; and we need to give the same kind of attentiveness to the other poems in this group. Hymns by the two among Herbert's predecessors, to whom he stands nearest in style and tone, are added for comparison; and a hymn very much in Herbert's manner, but adding a gently mystical conviction, by Henry Vaughan, his admirer and avowed disciple.

Notes

PRAISE (II)

Several titles, in *The Temple*, serve Herbert for more than one poem. This is the second *Praise*.

The very first couplet announces the two paradoxical sides to Herbert's faith that pervade all his poems: the Kingship of Christ ('How sweetly doth *My Master* sound! *My Master!*') and the unforced candour of personal access and personal relationship with Him.

For an approach to this poem different from that suggested in the critical commentary, it is worth seeing what has become of Psalm 116 in this transformation of it. Use the Prayer Book version, preferably.

Thou grew'st soft . . . this verse needs to be read aloud (indeed, sung if possible) for its point and nature to come fully home.

ANTIPHON (I)

Must bear the longest part . . . the reference is to part-singing in choir or madrigal consort. The certain meaning is 'chief, or most important part'—but 'fundamental part' would bring out the musical implication well. For probably the suggestion behind *longest* is of the most active part-line, containing the major proportion of sustained notes, a foundation for the harmony.

There is a sonnet by John Donne beginning *At the round earth's imagin'd corners sing*, and Herbert's cosmography here is worth pausing on.

VERTUE

The span of Herbert's life was the great age of the madrigal and air in English music. A glance at a few of the finest Elizabethan songs—by Campion, say, or Dowland—would make a good preliminary to this poem. (*See* E. H. Fellowes' *English Madrigal Verse, 1588–1632.*)

Sweet Spring . . . it is difficult for us to rescue, and respond freshly to, the key-word of this poem. It has gone soft for us. But the third verse insists that we try.

My musick shows . . . the verse-ending throughout the poem is itself a 'dying fall', an imitation of a cadence in music. Herbert makes delicate play with the situation. His metre has suggested musical possibilities; by implication he now requires the composer's collaboration. Between them, they point up the sense of the lines.

THE ELIXIR

There is no need of specialized knowledge in alchemy for a reading that will take the subtlety and edge of this poem. But the reader does need to grasp what the elixir was for the alchemists; and to gloss the technical terms carefully. If Ben Jonson's play can be called to mind, so much the better—it will keep one alert to the pursuit of riches implicit in so much 'popular' alchemy: and certainly Herbert has this in mind.

This is one of the poems that survives in an earlier version, and reveals both Herbert's skill in revision, and the care he took to revise and perfect his work. Originally the poem was called *Perfection*. The first verse read thus:

> Lord teach me to referr
> All things I doe to thee
> That I not onely may not err
> But allso pleasing be.

The second verse of our *Elixir* does not appear in *Perfection* at all. After our third verse comes one which Herbert deleted as a whole:

> He that does aught for thee,
> Marketh that deed for thine:

> And when the Divel shakes the tree,
> Thou saist, this fruit is mine.

The original final verse read thus:

> But these are high perfections:
> Happy are they that dare
> Lett in the Light to all their actions
> And show them as they are.

Herbert was dissatisfied and struck it through, and substituted the last verse we now have. There are losses in the final *Elixir*; but there are more than compensating gains. How characteristic of Herbert that, once he has the notion of alchemy, he makes it *transmute* the whole poem.

Not rudely, as a beast . . . the reader may find it worth looking up Hamlet's last soliloquy.

Which with his tincture . . . *his* has the force of the modern *its*. With this verse, compare the claim in Herbert's prose treatise, *The Country Parson*, 'Nothing is little in God's service: If it once have the honour of that Name, it grows great instantly.'

THE 23D PSALME

Herbert draws upon the Coverdale version in the Prayer Book, as well as upon the Authorized Version of the Bible. He makes use of the version in Sternhold and Hopkins's complete *Metrical Versions of the Psalms*.

The reader will prefer to make his own notes of Herbert's changes—every slight modification has its point. Though (characteristically) many hymn-books miss it out, Herbert does not balk at the harshness of verse 5: but observe how he transforms its vindictiveness with the suggestion of the communion table.

The versing of this psalm by Sidney appears next, inviting comparison. But there are other comparisons no less rewarding and fascinating that the reader may like to make: with Addison's version, representing the Augustan age, and with the Victorian hymn that may be all too familiar. Hymn-books will provide all the versions referred to here except Sidney's.

While he is mine . . . a modification of the verse from the *Song of Songs*, 'My beloved is mine, and I am his.' (ii. 16.)

thy staffe to bear . . . primarily, no doubt, 'to bear me up', provide me with support. There may be some suggestion of 'giving me my bearings'.

Philip Sidney's PSALM XXIII

The variety and the point of Sidney's metrical innovations in his paraphrases of the first forty psalms may well have suggested much to Herbert, and this is a fine example. But more than the delicate handling of metre and movement, the unassuming intimacy, the tenderness, of the tone of address, bring us close to the later poet.

Robert Southwell's NEW PRINCE, NEW POMPE

Southwell was a Jesuit priest who died, a martyr, in 1595. In discovering paradox and irony, as it were *inside* the Christian story, and eliciting these directly into meditative or devotional verse, Southwell has as good a claim as any to be the pioneer of divine poetry in this tradition. The note of frank homeliness in the poem chosen makes it apt for comparison with Herbert.

It is uncertain how the text should be printed—there is at present no established version of Southwell's poems. Some would reject the division into four-line stanzas and print the poem continuously.

Henry Vaughan's PEACE

Vaughan was a Welsh doctor, a convinced adherent of the Church, his faith illumined by mystical experience. He was a devoted admirer of Herbert, and modelled many of his divine poems directly upon those of his master. His first collection, *Silex Scintillans*, was published in 1650—his work belongs to a later period than Herbert's.

He is thy gracious friend . . . observe in such a couplet as this how a note like Herbert's is qualified by something very different.

II   His Quick-piercing Mind

Even in poems whose aim it is to remain song-like, susceptible of musical accompaniment, and therefore immediately expressive in a simple way, Herbert exacts from us an alert attention. So the poems we have read this far have suggested. The purpose of the group we come to now is to reflect the personal note that sounds in his work: what makes his poems peculiarly his own, and adds a distinctive flavour to English poetry. We find here some indication of his range of interests; of his methods as a poet; of his idiom, turn of phrase, and tones of speech. We are made sharply aware of a manner, a way with himself and others that affects us directly, and yet is not easy to sum up. It has candour, and a certain force; yet it is unassertive, it does not push the self forward; and yet again it is unreserved, unconcealing. The manner is before all else courteous. Herbert's kinship with Sir Philip Sidney goes deep. His is the manner, in a later age, of the perfect Elizabethan courtier, the gentle man, poised, assured yet deferential. He is God's courtier, and everyone's gentleman in His name. So we find in the poems a way of speech that is never rude or assertive or overbearing or ungallant (unless the poem is to bring to light, dramatize, and rebuke some failure in himself). We find an unfailing tact that we come to take for granted; but we can check upon it by looking again at the material Herbert handles in any one of the poems in this group—and reflecting upon the pitfalls, upon how easily a false note might have been struck, how tiny indelicacies could have marred all. We can detect the grace, the considerateness, the attitude of incipient tenderness, in phrase after phrase that open the poems:

> Busie enquiring heart, what wouldst thou know?
> Why dost thou prie,..

> Love bade me welcome: yet my soul drew back...

It would; it would draw back, expressing its embarrassed sense of 'pushing forward' by resuming modesty, claiming no status.

The character we feel in this verse is remarkably endowed with innate considerate courtesy; it is also endowed with intellectual bite, acute and varied interests, a wide and stored experience of men and affairs, introspective astuteness, and an unusual power of quizzical half-humorous self-regard. It is a character with an outgoing instinct to *feel* life, and get that life into language. These are general suggestions that the reader may wish to check against particular poems. But a further suggestion holds good for nearly all of them, and may prove a useful way into their individuality; you are always listening to a voice in a Herbert poem. His feeling for the variety of tone, of rhythm and impetus that belongs to the human voice, seems inexhaustible; and it is this, as much as anything, that creates for us the sense of immediacy, of presence, of actual human experience, as we read his poems now. Rarely, too, is a poem composed of one voice, even one voice in altering registers and paces. There comes the further jolt of dramatic actuality when another voice, when the divine Voice itself even, speaks to him, or interrupts his self-communing. And Herbert's command of the exactly appropriate tone or nuance for that other Voice is like a dramatist's or a novelist's: it vindicates the depth of his understanding of the whole situation out of which the voices speak. Consider, in this light, the voices of *The Quip*; or trace the changing tones through *Redemption* with its gentle but astonishing answering Voice which so overwhelms the raconteur that his tale abruptly ends.

A last suggestion for the reader to test out, first with the *Jordan* poems about the poet-priest's art, and then with others. What aligns Herbert not only with other, and greater, poets but also with faithful craftsmen in all skills and in all ages, is his dedication to perfect workmanship. The finest workmanship is for him the test of truth, of self-submission to a higher standard of total accuracy than any less skilled way with language exacts. In poem after poem, and at one point after another, we need to focus our attention with the enquiry, why is it so and not otherwise; for the answer, the most delicate and exact answer we can manage, will surely let us further into the truth the poem holds, into the kind of experience to be found there. Not only is Herbert—to judge simply by the range of interests and perceptions his imagery, vocabulary, and proverbial phrases exhibit —the very type of the creative and imaginative artist, 'a man on whom nothing is lost'; he also makes poems in which nothing is lost. Everything about his poem—its tone of voice, its metrical pattern, its rhythmical movement from line to line, its shape and size, its emblems and images—joins to become an *action* of its theme. Each poem is a small drama, and each facet of workmanship is an actor with some distinct rôle necessary for the whole. Rhymes, for instance, will constantly be found exerting a subtle pressure of their own: joining two reluctant partners, opposing concealed adversaries to one another, establishing relationships across the lines. Nor did Herbert find any of the more trivial skills of word-play too flippant to be brought into service now and again. He has a fine judgment of just what kind of poem to make, in order to explore, and offer in all clarity and distinctness in the sight of God, this or that experience, or act of faith, or hope. He was, we have to remember, a highly trained and gifted rhetorician; he knew the skills of manipulation, of persuasion and argument, of versification. The variety of his inventions and innovations just about matches the variety of his enquiries into the predicaments and moods of the devoted, yet always wayward, human spirit. Each poem becomes an emblem and an action of its theme.

Deniall, for example, is a poem (looking forward in this sense to those of our next section) of spiritual disappointment, of thwarted hope and a sense of uselessness. One look at the stanza-pattern is enough to suggest the pushes and pulls of the vexed, uneasy self. Take the third line of each verse—the prolonged one, where the complaint, the sense of grievance, gets its unhindered release. The first of them offers the clue to the metre and rhyming of the whole poem:

> Then was my heart broken, as was my verse:

Read aloud (as it has to be) the very line of statement has the nerveless 'broken' rhythm it speaks of; and it suggests how the disordered, unco-operative, unrhyming, irregularly rhythmed poem as a whole acts out the condition it speaks of. Looking down those third lines, we notice how nearly that of the fourth verse repeats that of the third: and indeed it is so with the verses as a whole. For Herbert's poetry has hold of that special attribute of the sense of vexed frustration—its tendency to repeat itself, the plaintiveness changing its terms ever so little, the whine remaining. An exact psychological touch: the key phrase, the gist of the complaint, at the end of each verse, doesn't even make the gesture of minor change. It insists. Then with the long line of the fifth verse a motion of self-rebuke comes in, a hint of 'a broken spirit, a broken and a contrite heart' which God will not despise:

> My feeble spirit, unable to look right,

And to speak that line is to feel a new rhythmical firmness, catching the natural bent of the line-length, preparatory for the last verse, whose clear, deliberate

> That so thy favours granting my request

feels right at last.

This is one way—there are others—of tracing out in its movement the poem's establishment of order and patience in the dispirited self, by establishing the order implicit in the stanza's pattern, though obscured at first. The home-thrust, of course, is the dedication of rhyme to the same purpose. The denial of a final expected rhyme at the end of a verse has a peculiarly strong effect; it leaves a door open, it fails to clinch the issue, it is more fuddling than the mere denial of a rhyme *en route*. Herbert's refusals of that end-rhyme take varied and pointed forms. The first refusing word—*disorder*—gives us the significance of the refusals; and, a three-syllable, light-ending, hard word against the expected single-syllable rhyme with *eares*, it judders the rhythm at the same moment as it defeats *our* 'eares' by denying what they expect. Different subtleties work towards a similar dislocation (with a heavy-ending word) in the second stanza; but the repeated refusals of the middle two stanzas affect us more directly, through the lameness of the final word against the rhyme-expectations, through its appeal to *our* 'hearing', and through the simultaneous collapse of the verbal rhythms into inertness, indolence. *Discontented*, in the last stanza but one, has a wilful edge to its refusal. We feel a sort of perverse game by now; an enjoyment of being awkward. So the effect at the end of the last stanza, and the end of the wilful poem, is masterly. The ear and the nervous system are set at rest together as we listen and feel; the 'normal' pattern of rhythm, cadence, and rhyme establishes itself—and we say 'normal' because underneath the disturbed surface, all along, we have felt its inevitable coming. To the last word, the *action* of the poem is as much a matter of what the words say, and mean, as what they do. For *chime* has a double point. It speaks at once of a *rhythmical* togetherness, and a *harmonious* unison: and then again, it evokes the peal of bells that rings to devotion, it calls upon deep, instinctive habits— even if, from time to time, devotion fails to bring its expected peace of mind. This delicate wit, working through the very grain of our language, we need to detect in such phrases as *heartlesse breast*, and *silent eares*, and *thunder of alarms*. And as we take to ourselves the force and point of the images, we need to alert ourselves especially to the treating of music and the sense of hearing. That is the sense called into play by a poetry of rhyme-denial: and when the penultimate stanza gives us the discarded lute, we recollect that music, in Herbert's day, was not only a deep joy and consolation ('my heaven on earth' he himself called it) but veritably a type of heaven, a re-creation of the Divine Order, the music of the circling spheres, the music that restores King Lear, and celebrates the return of Portia to Belmont. The soul *untun'd, unstrung* is unprepared to recreate that Divine Harmony, or to partake in it. Like a *nipt blossome* (how sharp and painful the *nipt* feels alongside the fullness of *blossome*—but what a salutary reduction of scale, too: the soul mustn't be encouraged to think of itself under comparisons too lofty) it is unable to *look right*, to be itself in nature.

The poem, as a poem, never doubts that Order, that nature; never doubts that the divine answer will come, when it will come. The implied pattern beneath the disturbed stanza waits patiently—observing the distractions and vexations of the sorry and wilful human spirit—for the time of mending. Nor has this discussion at all exhausted the varieties of that pattern; nor even touched upon the variety of vocal tone and nuance: there is much attention still to be focussed.

The three poems added to this group for comparison, and to suggest a context in which to set the personal note of Herbert, are chosen not for any likeness to Herbert, but for achievements of 'character' quite different from his. They share—Donne's, especially—the dedication of technique to acting out what the poem affirms; but they will serve to bring home what variety of style and character found a place in the tradition.

Notes

DENIALL

Untun'd, unstrung . . . it would be worth looking up Ulysses' speech on Order, and its reference to music, to feel the full suggestion of this image. (*Troilus and Cressida*, I. 3)

O cheer and tune . . . a 'packed' line if ever there was one in Herbert; best to pause over the verbs.

JORDAN (1)

Herbert's placing of the name of the river Jordan above his two poems about the poet's art has more than one significance. It is the river of Grace in which the Christian poet bathes, as against the Helicon of pagan inspiration. The crossing of it is the traditional symbol of complete conversion, or accepted redemption. And (2 *Kings*, v, should be consulted) that river is the source of true cleanliness, a washing away of all defilement.

It may well be a mistake to read this poem as an 'attack' upon this school or that; on fantastic or decorative or witty and ingenious styles; on conventional forms of courtly love poetry, or any others. Herbert's moral is for himself; Jordan is *his* experience. His protest, if protest it is, seems to be against the usurpation by love poets of the whole realm of poetic art. There are other claims to be staked out—and a language appropriate for those claims.

sudden arbours . . . the art of the designer of gardens and landscapes lay partly in taking the viewer by surprise with an unexpected enclosure.

Who plainly say . . . 'There is for this writer another way, which he announces with all the exaggeration of a convert.' (L. Martz.) This is an equivocal, humorous poem (in one of its aspects), and evidently not a manifesto. The next *Jordan* poem modifies its pronouncements a little—and so does the finest of Herbert's poetry!

THE QUIP

There's no finer poem, for a study of Herbert's dramatic mastery in handling the voice.

Then came quick Wit . . . but we don't in fact *hear* him. It is a metrical touch we have here, one of Herbert's most delightful.

DIALOGUE

But when all my care . . . nothing the poor wretch can do (for himself) will make the possession of his soul a 'positive asset'—one gets the point best by using modern business-transaction jargon.

Get without repining . . . to whom does the *repining* apply?

My glorie and desert . . . as we find in Marvell's *Coy Mistress*, the word was pronounced, and often spelt, *desart*.

GIDDINESSE

And snudge in quiet . . . this fine old word means both 'to remain snug and quiet' and 'to be stingy, having one's gains for oneself'.

Like a Dolphins skinne . . . 'a fish like a mackerel; its metallic colours undergo rapid changes on its being taken out of the water and about to die, but it cannot be inferred that the changes have any relation to its *desires*'. (Canon Hutchinson.)

Thou make us dayly . . . 2 *Corinthians*, iv. 16, may be consulted.

REDEMPTION

The poem takes the form of a sonnet, and it uses the mode (in part) of allegory: in both these ways, it would have seemed 'old-fashioned'. What happens, therefore, as the quiet matter-of-fact voice explaining a legal transaction becomes tense with the frustrations of the search is the more moving and disturbing against the old-fashioned framework.

Notice that the conventions of a legal document are preserved even in the poignant final words, and consider how those two words, thus spelt, act upon one another.

HOPE

'One can accept the poem without plunging deeply into its meaning, because of the bump with which the short lines, giving the flat, poor, surprising answer of reality, break the momentum of the long hopeful lines in which a new effort has been made. The movement is so impeccable as to be almost independent of the meaning of the symbols.

'And, indeed, the symbols themselves seem almost to be used in a way familiar to the mathematician; as when a set of letters may stand for any numbers of a certain sort, and you are not curious to know which numbers are meant because you are only interested in the relations between them. . . .' (Empson.)

This is an ideal starting-point for experiencing the poem, and the reader is urged not to consult what follows, nor to continue reading the remarkably suggestive discussion in Empson's *Seven Types of Ambiguity*, until the poem has been directly enjoyed, its images felt and taken to heart, and allowed to speak for themselves.

a watch . . . the brevity of human time? the regular speed with which time passes? that the time for fulfilment of hopes is overdue?—the last suggestion has particularly the implication of the delicate *hint*, so right in point of manners for the poem's courtesy.

an anchor . . . the need to endure, to hold on for a long time yet —and, perhaps, to expect little progress or movement? And is it, perhaps, the certain hope of redemption, or of resurrection—in view of the watch?

an old prayer-book . . . for the prayers used in regular and constant devotions? for the ordered routine of spiritual life?

an optick . . . is it the faith that searches the heavens? or an aid to descry help afar off? or the far distance at which hope's fulfilments remain? or the eyes lifted from close poring over that prayer-book towards rare illumination?

a viall full of tears . . . of repentance? or of sorrow and pain for long-delayed fulfilment? or of regret for this world's pleasures, renounced to so little apparent purpose?

a few green eares . . . each reply seems more pointed, yet enigmatic. Is this an equally delicate hint of present spiritual immaturity, delightfully coupled with the promise of harvest to come?

a ring . . . the perfect sign of eternity (which Vaughan saw 'like a great Ring'); and, perhaps, of union with God, or through His Church, with Christ—remember how the *Song of Songs* was still interpreted at this time. Empson suggests—and it quickens one's feeling for the poem, indeed—that a halo may be intended here, too; and that Herbert projects as the speaker one whose disappointment has not put him past vanity.

The anchor was itself an emblem of Hope, traditionally, in Herbert's time.

SINNES ROUND

As with *Deniall*, there is a dedicated artifice in this poem easy to appreciate; and, as with *Deniall*, that is only a starting-point. The poem is a very subtle one.

The Sicilian Hill ... Mount Etna.

This poem makes an admirable study for those interested in the range and thrust of Herbert's diction.

JORDAN (II)

The first and third of Sidney's Sonnets to Stella should be read alongside this poem. Professor Martz goes so far as to call it 'a superb example of sacred parody'. The poem was originally titled *Invention* (see glossary).

This poem ought not to be read simply as a recantation, an abandonment of rhetorical skills, a renunciation of Donne and a choice for Sidney: any more than *Jordan* (I) should be read simply as an attack. It is a colloquy with the self about the nature, and the difficulty, of sincerity; and about the *temptations* that skill in eloquence, and subtlety of mind and imagination, bring with them. To 'weave my self into the sense' for Herbert meant vanity, and a tainting of real understanding. Poetry, which should be self-forgetfulness, becomes self-glorification.

How wide is all this ... Wide of the mark; and at the same time, like a cavity, empty.

LOVE

The taking of a meal together as the traditional expression of true friendship, as well as the communion table of the altar, underlies the climax of this poem. The extraordinary fineness of its courtesies makes it apt for study alongside *The Collar*: each illuminates the other in point of the significance of manners. The reader may like to pass by the three poems in between, and go straight to the far extreme of rudeness—still at the communion table—with 'I struck the board . . .'

Thomas Carew's LINES FOR MARIA WENTWORTH

Carew was a courtier and diplomat, poet and wit, who died in 1640. Nearly all of his verse is secular—love poetry for the most part; blending the elegance and refinement of the line of Ben Jonson with the sharpness and daring of mind and imagination characteristic also of Donne and Herbert.

John Donne's HOLY SONNET X

John Donne, like Herbert, passed from a brilliant and varied youth, in which remarkable endowments of mind and personality revealed themselves, through a gradual change of heart that led eventually to his taking Holy Orders. In the Church he rose to eminence, and as Dean of St. Paul's was the most celebrated, and the finest, preacher of his day. He is the pre-eminent metaphysical poet—not least because of the range of his styles and interests. His poems extend from the most flippant and cynical love-jests to the most anguished and personal religious meditations.

Holy Sonnet X has been chosen to suggest a force of personality, and a passion of mind and imagination, far exceeding Herbert's. But it is as much an action of its theme as any of Herbert's poems, and needs excited, concentrated attention.

Henry Vaughan's THE MORNING WATCH

At first reading, perhaps, impetuous exaltation quieting itself to humble prayer may seem the whole of this poem. But its shape reveals itself as carefully and meaningfully woven—a metric that, like so many of Herbert's, subtly controls the direction of thought and feeling. The poem has been chosen, and set next to Donne's, to bring home what widely different poetic temperaments found ways to express themselves in the 'Divine Poetry' of the age.

III The Many Spiritual Conflicts

When we have studied sensitively enough the two *Jordan* poems, we know that the dedication of his heart and skill to the making of a true poem was not a simple matter for Herbert. It wasn't only an aesthetic matter either. It meant a moral struggle, a struggle to achieve what we easily call sincerity, no doubt, but much more a struggle to achieve sincerity before God; a realization of what in the last resort, with all pretences and disguises shed, the self actually is, and is like. His earlier verse had been officially dedicated to heaven; but, in recollection, and seen in present perspective, seemed made of sought-after 'quaint words and trim inventions', and of 'thoughts that burnisht, sprouted, swelld'. Pause on that *swelld*: we feel the sense of ostentation, of vanity. And then—'*curling* with metaphor a plain intention, decking the sense. . . .' 'Curling' has the suggestion of an aristocratic veneer, of the nobility's elegant self-adornment, and the fop's varnished surface. With that marked change in the tone of voice which we have learned to note as enacting the moment of clearer discovery, Herbert discerns the stain in such *eloquent* 'dedication', the pride in the self-conscious skilfulness:

> As flames do work and winde, when they ascend,
> So did I weave my self into the sense.
> But while I bustled, I might heare a friend
> Whisper, How wide is all this long pretence!
> There is in love a sweetness readie penn'd:
> Copie out onely that, and save expense.

If the lines propose for ideal a simplicity costly to achieve and only rarely given to a poet to achieve, they also take us into the subtle ways of the deceiving heart. Ascent is the right direction, and the image of the altar there reminds us of the kind of offering up of his art that Herbert desires. But even in that act there is 'winding', there are the spiralling self-deceptions and cheats of the ascending spirit tainted with self-concern, pride, reflected glory. Subtlety of metaphor and spiritual vanity are felt as facets of a single danger; and that very danger cannot be separated from the effort of dedication, the will to make the poetry pure and total, and everything a poem can be. As Rosamund Tuve has it in those pages of her *A Reading of George Herbert* that deal with the *Jordan* poems (they are among the best in the book), 'The true and complete absence of self-deceit which Herbert achieves, he achieves by rooting out of himself every vestige of self-seeking; by a submission of his will to the will of Christ his master.'

So we make now the natural move from poems in which we may have interested ourselves primarily in acts of technical 'wholeness' and dedication, to the group of poems that illustrate what is humanly most representative and important in his achievement. These are the poems of inner conflict, of coming to terms with himself; poems that elicit from the proud and unruly will a readiness to accept the chosen way, with all its disappointments. The here and now, to which we feel his verse to be so faithful, is the experience of which all of us know some reflection, in some measure. There is the feeling of dryness and uselessness, there is the tempting desire for what cannot in the nature of things be had, there is rebellion against the limits set by illness, and moodiness, and incapacity, there is the failure of faith when the very choice of vocation depends on faith's stability. The essay on Herbert by L. C. Knights, in *Explorations*, is the most suggestive account to study by way of preparation for a full grasp upon these poems. Professor Knights sees Herbert as using his poetic art to explore, adjust himself to, and resolve, his difficulties and conflicts: conflicts that turn upon the need for submission of the merely personal will, and the need for rejection of the wrong kinds of success, and of temptations to cheat disappointment by dreams of what might have been. He sees the poems as a way for Herbert to accept himself for what he is, failures and weaknesses admitted.

It is here, perhaps, that the poems may touch any of us to the quick. *Affliction (I)* or *Affliction (IV)*, two of Herbert's supreme achievements, though marvellously sure and sober, give us the raw grind of dejection and discontent with the self and its lot. Yet still the art controlling the verse is a dedicated art, an instrument of the tenacity that will absolutely hold to the hard, sharp truth of feeling and perception. The art is an instrument of insight, of clarification, directed particularly upon 'coming to terms with oneself', appraising a situation that is difficult anyway, and may be painful. Herbert's habitual honesty, his self-giving into poetry produces, we find throughout these poems, two apparently contrary effects. The moods of despair, rebellion, or vexation get the freest possible play, they seem to happen all over again in the words of the poem. Yet at the same time they are in the past; the poem of the present moment is an achievement of re-direction, renewal, submission. By its very character as a poem it offers a guarantee—maybe only the guarantee of faith—that the mood is not the reality; the reality (as in the wonderful *Pilgrimage*) is a step beyond.

Let us look, in this light, at *The Collar*: the most dramatic of all, though perhaps less profoundly moving than the *Affliction* poems, *The Flower*, and *The Pilgrimage*. The poem is best read after *Love*, so that the rudeness, the lapse of characteristic manners, at the outset shall make its full effect. There are three distinct shocks. There's the dramatic shock of the action itself—'I struck the board'—as an opening to a poem; there's the verbal shock of the blasphemy—the board was the altar, the Lord's Table; and there's the shock of the personal lapse in the author of (say) *Love*—the lack of breeding, poise, consideration. It is important to appreciate this unHerbertian rudeness, for it is a clue to the real drama going on. What first strikes us is turbulent rebellion, checked by the sudden address of the Voice, and a resumption of childlike faith. The Divine Father calls, the rebellious priest remembers who He is, and answers with the formal deference naturally owing to a father (in Herbert's time) and to God: 'My Lord.' Yet that does not wholly describe what happens. There is present in the subtle, pointed organization of the words and the lines a sharp, undeceived watcher who knows from the brash start that the *real* childishness is *in* the turbulent rebellion, the bad manners, the violent demands for freedom. Let us look down the poem. What does the freedom mean but irresponsibility, unbounded self-indulgence, no restrictions, no restraints, a purposeless and incoherent living that really is 'loose as the wind'? This growing up that the poem acts out, the realizing what the outburst and the behaviour are really like, we may feel in every aspect of the poetic art *except* the buoyant, crude, outspoken, vigorous, challenging, angry, gusty tone of voice. Are we to read the poem accepting that tone as manly and responsible, the tone of someone who no longer 'winks and does not see'? Yes, partly—for that is certainly how it takes itself. And to that, we shall hear the final 'Child' putting revolting nature and hot temper unforgettably in their place. The energy of the poem will have so caught our rebellious and gusty instincts into itself, that we experience the whole thing alongside the unmannerly banger of tables. There is the Voice to respond to. But there is also the poem that contains the Voice. Any poem of Herbert, we have found by now, acts as if to focus something perfectly; the bad-mannered outburst, the physical intrusion (like people who bang doors), and the tacit blasphemy of the priest at the altar, are here perfectly in focus. We have to respond to that focussing, that clarification, too.

Take, for instance, the organization of the metre. We are aware at first only of the surge and thrust, of the jab and taunt of the Voice, all the impetuosity of speech, thriving on its own rhythms of temper and release. Yet controlling that surge and thrust, presenting it for our more sensitive understanding (and for his more sensitive humility), there is an organization of extreme skill. Only when the divine Voice can make itself heard does the metrical pattern at last assert itself. (That Voice, we notice, will not have the ungracious manners to interrupt, it will wait even for the garrulousness of undirected rebellion to say its say.) There it is at the end: a four-line stanza, of 10 syllables, 4 syllables, 8 syllables, and 6 syllables, rhyming *abab*. Up to that point, the poet's scrutinizing art has so arranged the ingredients of the pattern as to form the most extreme lack of regularity compatible with the survival of even the dimmest outline. The stanza-pattern is quite submerged in all the flurry and bustle. The rhymes go astray. We get as many as five consecutive unrhymed lines—when spiritual muddle and discord is at its height. We get internal instead of line-ending rhymes—they have lost their place. We find such notions as 'My lines and life are free; free as the rode' acting out their freedom by expanding ridiculously beyond the due metrical allowance. Herbert's lines—his verses— are free indeed. Sharp observation will reveal that almost every rhyme-link has its special point, in relation either to its defiance of the eventual *abab*, or to its occurring when the syllabic movement defies its eventual 10—4—8—6. Why, for instance, is that 'sigh and pine' of the wide open mouth kept waiting seven lines for a rhyme? So that at last, when really dry, the rhyming 'wine Before my sighs did dry it' may be offered.

But what *wine* is this? No sooner have we taken the suggestion from this ridiculously (and childishly) jumbled and tangled metric, that only the divine Voice at the end can straighten out, than the images and emblems, which we thought just part of the loud-mouthed protests, begin to pinch. Harvest: thorn: blood: wine: grain—the homely language of gospel parable, pulpit homily, and sacrament. He struck the board, but it is still the Board, present throughout the poem (though almost lost to sight and consciousness in the noise); and the body and blood of our Lord are still the bread and the wine. They are tossed about to worldly and self-indulgent purposes by the gusty voice, yet remain recognizably themselves. As the thorns become a crown, and the grain of seed dies to bring forth fruit (cordial, indeed, for the heart), so by merely *being* there, and long before the rebellious spirit can hear, they also say 'Child'. The very images of the

poem, as well as the disordered metric, and the jumbled rhymes
—like subtle but strong undercurrents—are saying it from the
start, 'Child'.

Meantime the vocabulary and the other images act out their
side of the recognition, and the rebuke, no less energetically.
After the bread and wine of the board come the flowers and
garlands of the courtly and gay world; but they don't last.
'Blasted' hadn't then quite the rude, derisive force it has for us, but
it begins a lurch towards vulgarity and offensiveness in diction,
which is loose and free in another sense. The speech coarsens.
There is the nasty insinuating tone of 'There is fruit, and thou
hast hands'; there is the hinted but unuttered 'fly-blown' behind
'sigh-blown'; there are the peremptory shouts about the death's-
head; there are indecorous images, the reverse of courtly, in the
cage, the rope of sands (he can't even make a sensible metaphor
now, who once taught rhetoric at Cambridge). The vulgarity of
diction, phrase, and image is complete—*and childish*. 'Forsake
thy cage' is all very well. Collars, as well as being 'fits of anger',
'emblems of religious devotion', and 'emblems of the restraints
of conscience' were used in the taming of wild animals, and used
for them when tamed. They were used for madmen, too. And
by the time we get to that cage, the grain of the poetry will have
us enquire whether this rebellious spirit is coming from it or
going towards it. Is he 'slipping the collar' (a proverbial phrase
of the time) or showing how badly he needs one?

Each aspect of the poetry's focussing art, then, has suggested
something of the childishness *in* the rebellion. Notice how the
poem's conclusion sharpens the focus still further. Much though
you may wish to, you cannot in fact read it aloud, sensitively,
and make the intrusion of the Voice sudden and devastating. For
that Voice, and the answer, come at the end of the firm and
ordered stanza, not at the beginning. And the beginning fore-
stalls the Voice, with a difficult recognition, a statement of painful clarity: 'But as I rav'd, and grew more fierce and wilde at
every word.' The poem has, so to speak, focussed its experience
for him, too; he has to recognize where the childishness lay,

where the irresponsibility. And the qualm of recognition comes (doesn't it always?) a split second before the Other Voice speaks. The word that chimes with 'Child' is the word that recognizes the whole outburst for what it was—'wilde'.

And yet how compelling, how real the rebellion is. To read the poem again now is still to be caught up in the tempestuous mood—for is there not something valid about it? Isn't there a place for anger and rebellion? We have to live the tension over and over again. Yet it oughtn't to escape us, however we answer that question, that Herbert truly becomes himself again in the last phrase. He remembers his manners; remembers, in the double sense, his station in life; remembers—if we may cast his own pun back upon him—his table manners. He is once more the priest at the altar. He has not simply abandoned the temptation to unrestrained and worldly success and become a child again; he has also seen the childishness in turbulent and unruly desires and in irresponsible liberty, and become himself—very much a grown-up.

It would be misleading to suggest that other poets of the age offer a poetry of conflict quite comparable with Herbert's; for the sort of poems we have in this group represent precisely Herbert's uniqueness. But it could be useful to look back to Donne's *Batter my Heart*, and to read his *Hymne to God the Father*, the better to distinguish other depths of conflict, and a more immediate sense of anguish; and then, to set a mark on the opposite side of Herbert's verse, to read Marvell's *Dialogue*, where the conflict has something of the character of a game of chess. The opposing forces are drawn up for battle, their relative strengths gauged; yet no real battle is joined. It is delicate and urbane, but not altogether untroubled. From the duet comes a quiet, bitter recognition of human limitations, soul and body each imposing restraints and limits upon the other, not far from Herbert's kinds of recognition.

Notes

THE COLLAR

Me thoughts I heard . . . 'At one time I felt that in this well-known ending Herbert was evading the issue by simply throwing up the conflict and relapsing into the naive simplicity of childhood. But of course I was wrong. The really childish behaviour is the storm of rage in which the tempestuous desires—superbly evoked in the free movement of the verse—are directed towards an undefined "freedom". What the poem enforces is that to be "loose as the wind" is to be as incoherent and purposeless; that freedom is to be found not in some undefined "abroad", but, in Ben Jonson's phrase, "here in my bosom, and at home".' (L. C. Knights.)

It is worth taking a good look at the poem as it stands on the page; taking it in with the eye.

THE CROSSE

The title seems to have a double force; both that made explicit in the last stanza turning upon the desire sufficiently to serve and do honour to the Christ who suffered; and that implicit in the notion that each has his cross to bear. Herbert's is his weakness and sickness of body: and it was a most real cross to his proud and able spirit.

The poem has close affinities with *The Collar*, and is here set next to it deliberately. 'Herbert's "cunning bosome-sinne" of discontent, due to the frustrations arising from his ill body, is explored in all its ramifications, with blasphemous murmurings and bitter accusations against God's justice; but concluding, like *The Collar*, in a whiplash of self-control and conformity with God's will.' (L. Martz.)

And lay my threatnings . . . Probably, as Professor Martz suggests, the word relates to the old verb *threap*, meaning 'to offer, positively and insistently'.

Of the first three stanzas Professor Martz remarks, most suggestively:

'But already the poem is revealing the true source of the speaker's trouble: there is far too much insistence on the "I" and the "my" and the "me"—fourteen times in three short stanzas. The note of personal wilfulness is emphasized by the scarcely covert pride in "all my wealth and familie"—think of how all this might have added to God's honour! And then the human wilfulness comes out into the open in a tone of self-indulgent petulance, with an effect of deliberate ironic awareness:

> Besides, things sort not to my will,
> Ev'n when my will doth studie thy renown . . .

But suddenly, in three lines at the close, the whole edifice of self-will collapses, as we have known it would.'

With but foure words, my words . . . words, that is, that I now take to myself, and make mine.

CONFESSION

And fall, like rheumes . . . Bacon has it that 'If there be any weak or affected part, this is sufficient to draw rheums, or humours, to it.'

The first and third verses provide fine examples of Herbert's command of movement—his control of line-ending, and the stir of a phrase across the metre, so as to place the weight where it is needed, or make the voice *do* what it says. Examine the mole's activity, for instance: or the secrecies of the first verse.

Onely an open breast . . . a deliberate paradox, of the sort embedded in traditional Christian teaching, but 'turned' by Herbert very much to his own uses.

I challenge here . . . 'I challenge for clarity and brightness the brightest day and the clearest diamond; at their best they shall seem opaque and overcast compared with my heart, once cleared by confession.' Thus the prose sense. But the imagery will reward a more sensitive appreciation.

CONSCIENCE

'Busie old foole, unrulie Sunne' is the opening to one of Donne's most buoyant love poems.

Observe the meaningful subtleties of rhyme connections, and sound-patterns, in the first stanza—there is probably no more skilful verse in all Herbert.

The ever-nagging, self-consciously finicky and particular conscience, that conscience which can be a source of spiritual pride, and the death of joy, is the conscience addressed.

AFFLICTION (I)

There are two discussions of this poem that the reader should take care to consult. One—Empson's in *Seven Types of Ambiguity*—explores Herbert's use of paradox in the final couplet, in the light of the poem as a whole. The other occupies the central pages of L. C. Knight's chapter on Herbert in *Explorations*.

When first thou didst entice . . . 'In the masterly verse of *Affliction I* we have one of the most remarkable records in the language of the achievement of maturity and of the inevitable pains of the process. In the opening stanzas, movement and imagery combine to evoke the enchanted world of early manhood. But implicit in the description—as we see from "entice" and "entwine" and the phrase "argu'd into hopes"—is the admission that there *is* enchantment, an element of illusion. . . .' (L. C. Knights.)

The reader may profitably take up the clue of attention to the verbs that beset the poet, specially in the 7th stanza.

Psalm 31 (in the Prayer Book version) should be read as implied background to the whole poem; especially to its end.

My flesh began unto my soul . . . the verb is used idiomatically in the biblical way—'began to say'. The next three lines, with their verbs in the present tense, speak for the flesh.

My friends die . . . the deaths of so many of his influential friends and patrons played a significant part in that period of depression and crisis which preceded Herbert's resolve to take orders. (See introductory biography.)

Whereas my birth and spirit . . . after a succession of stanzas giving us the sense of pain, weakness, and despair with such immediacy, we have an equally direct expression of the sense of inner division and doubt. The 'prose sense' of these stanzas needs careful elucidation.

Yet me from my wayes taking . . . observe the rôle of the personal pronoun in the 'drama' of this poem.

Ah my deare God . . . the paradox is of the kind deliberately to bring the reader—and the speaker—up sharp. We do well to *start* by holding tenaciously to the primary meaning. Canon Hutchinson puts it thus: 'If he cannot hold on to his love of God even when he feels forsaken and unrewarded, he had better not hope to love at all.'

But we keep a little closer to Herbert's formulation, perhaps, by emphasizing that to love God is the proper end and function of the human spirit, it is blessedness: but that condition cannot come, save in love of God for His own sake—purely. To paraphrase, 'Let me not enjoy the blessed privilege of loving thee, unless I love thee for thy own sake, through every trial, and with no other desire or motive than to love thee.'

Compare the ends of some of the later sonnets of Sidney: notably Sonnet 61.

AFFLICTION (IV)

Both the *Affliction* poems will reward a reader's concern with their shape and metrical pattern, their 'order'.

My thoughts are all . . . 'He would often say, *He had a Wit like a Pen-Knife in a narrow sheath, too sharp for his Body.*' (Walton's

Life.) This second verse holds very contrary feelings and impulses in balance together; the images need careful attention. Note how the word *scatter'd* is picked up later in the poem.

Till I reach heav'n . . . this last line should be compared with the last line of *Affliction* (I): each illuminates the other.

THE PEARL

'*The Pearl* is addressed to God, but the speaker is a courtier who hardly acknowledges the object of his address for the first three stanzas. In them he proclaims his knowledge of the ways of Learning, Honour and Pleasure, the courtly trinity, with his rejection implied only in the refrain line. The speech is witty, proving the knowledge, and the accents are proper to such speech. But after the rhetorical descriptions, the poem abandons courtly boasting for grave address. The heightened speech of the conclusion finally establishes the iambic norm. The resolution of the last two lines is all the more conclusive after the daring rhythmical evocation of the labyrinths.' (J. H. Summers.)

The reference to St. Matthew's Gospel, xiii. 45, is given alongside the poem's title. Herbert meant that it should be consulted.

The head and pipes . . . it would be characteristic of Herbert to shift the metaphor from the wine-press to the printing-press. The *head* may be the fountain of knowledge, the universities; and the *pipes* the learned professions.

In vies of favour . . . 'I know how to gauge by the rules of courtesy who wins in a contest of doing favours; when each party is urged by ambition to do all he can by look or deed to win the world and bind it on his back.'

I know the wayes of Pleasure . . . *Pleasure*, for Herbert, comes out as the delight of music. With true rhetorical dexterity he chooses terms of musical skill and learning that can take on the sensuous implications of Pleasure. *Strains* describe lengths of tune in old dance forms; *relishes* are ornaments, or embellishments of accented notes, in interpreting music at the virginals, in song, or on the lute; *propositions* are like statements of theme that open a fugue, and await their *riposta*, or counter-statements; *lullings* refer to gentle refrains of the lullaby kind, in folk music.

THE FLOWER

It seems likely that in the original order Herbert planned for the poems of *The Temple*, this moving expression of a sense of new life arising from the shrivelled, dried-up state of weakness, irresolution, or despair, came after *The Crosse*.

Observe the grace and naturalness of the speaking voice at the opening of stanzas 1 and 2. The quiet, and glad, recognition—that seasons of dryness must be, that there *are* other months than May—which these two stanzas achieve—is unlike any note sounded in the poems read hitherto.

Making a chiming of a passing-bell . . . instead of the single tone of the funeral bell, the varied and heart-easing sound of the bells being chimed (swung just enough to make the clappers strike). *Chiming* always carries, though, the further senses suggested in the glossary.

This or that is . . . 'is' with force: is, in itself, or unchangeably; truly *exists*.

What frost to that? . . . 'There is no frost to compare with thy *least frown*; Arctic cold is nearer to the heat of the torrid zone than to such a frost.'

THE PILGRIMAGE

At the start of his fine discussion of the third stanza of this poem, with its manifold implications turning upon the word *Passion*, Professor Empson excellently suggests the distinguishing virtue of the whole poem: 'Its tone, prosaic, arid, without momentum, whose contrast with the feeling and experience conveyed gives a prophetic importance to this flat writing; there is the same even-voiced understatement in the language of the Gospels. This is made possible because, in the apparent story, he adopts the manner of a traveller, long afterwards, mentioning where he has been, and what happened to him, as if only to pass the time.'

The marvellously sensitive handling of the chosen stanza-form should be studied, as well as the changing tones of voice. What, for instance, should we make of the short tailing-off lines at each stanza-ending?

Cave of Desperation . . . it is important to enter in imagination into an attitude of belief that regarded Despair as a dangerously sinful condition.

At length I got unto the gladsome hill . . . 'The fourth verse, making skilful use of the varied lengths of line, and of the slight end-of-line pauses, reproduces the sensations of the traveller, as expectation—rather out of breath, but eager and confident—gives way abruptly to flat disappointment.' (L. C. Knights.)

So I flung away . . . We are made to feel this last, strong upsurge of the rebellious impulses of *The Collar*, just before the Voice speaks. This last verse is mysterious, and not at all easy to penetrate.

John Donne's A HYMNE TO GOD THE FATHER

Just as in the previous poem, full understanding at one point turns on our knowing how in the seventeenth century *wild* and *wold*, willed and would, are linked in oral pronunciation; so with this poem, the link between Donne and *done* is vital.

No reader who cares for music, and is interested even in slightly later settings to music of the Divine Poetry of this period, should miss an opportunity to hear Pelham Humfries' beautiful setting of the *Hymne to God the Father*. It has been recorded by Alfred Deller. See also the remarks on Donne's love for Church music, in Walton's *Life*.

The poem was written, probably, during Donne's illness of 1623, from which he did not expect to recover.

I have a sinne of feare . . . as at the opening of *The Pilgrimage*, we must recollect that such despair as this is a sinful condition.

Andrew Marvell's A DIALOGUE

Andrew Marvell was born in Hull in 1618. He took his degree at Trinity College, Cambridge, and was a tutor, a minor civil servant, and a politician, his life spanning the period of Cromwell's rule. He may be seen as the last great 'metaphysical' poet, and the one who most creatively drew into one poetic style the line of Ben Jonson and the line of Donne. He died in 1678. The reader may wish to consult T. S. Eliot's fine essay on his poetry.

IV Poetry of Meditation

'Prayer, or thought, or studying the stars,' wrote D. H. Lawrence in *Etruscan Places*, 'or watching the flight of birds, or studying the entrails of the sacrifice, it is all the same process ultimately, of divination. All it depends on is the amount of *true*, sincere, religious concentration you can bring to bear on your object. An act of pure attention, if you are capable of it, will bring its own answer. And you choose that object to concentrate upon which will best focus your consciousness. Every real discovery made, every serious and significant decision ever reached, was reached and made by divination. The soul stirs, and makes an act of pure attention, and that is a discovery.' It is good, at this point, to encounter a modern mind, and one of genius, reflecting on the process of meditation; for if, indeed, the tradition and methods of meditation are now largely lost to us, something humanly important is lost, too. 'The soul stirs, and makes an act of pure attention.' It is a perfect evocation of the poem of meditation; in Herbert's work, the fine flower of that faith whose difficult winning and holding we have been exploring. The pure attention, focussed upon the object which will best focus it, was in Herbert's time a long-practised discipline; its origins lay more with the Jesuit community than in any other one place, but in varied forms it was common, by the seventeenth century, to dedicated men and women of most Christian communities in Europe.

Briefly summed up, meditation acted like this. After due preparation and quiet, imagination works through the senses to 'compose' a scene, an incident, a character, a symbol, a theme, making it immediately present to the consciousness. Then, by the exercise of the understanding, its significance is explored, its meanings and truths set forth. Finally, by a responsive exercise of the affections, the desires, and the will, that meaning and truth enjoins its consequences upon the moral being, upon the heart. There is a renewal of the power of right action, and the disposition conforms itself to follow where mind working upon imagination has shown the way.

So pervasive is this basic structure in the divine poetry of the period that Professor Martz, in *The Poetry of Meditation* (which provides a helpful guide to the poems of this section), suggests that his term might be more valid as a classification than the rather bewildering 'Metaphysical Poetry' now hallowed by long usage. Look back, for example, now, to Southwell's *New Prince, New Pompe*. The structure of formal meditation is exactly worked out. Not that mere formal obedience to the rules, Ignatian or any other, is likely to be of itself a creative factor in poetry. But when the gift is there (as with Southwell, or Herbert), and when in the process of meditation the soul truly 'stirs, and makes an act of pure attention', there are indeed the conditions for poetry. For energetic imagination, acute mental exploration, an honest colloquy between mind and heart and an achievement of balance and integration, are (we have seen) of the very essence of meditation; and at the same time they can be ingredients of poetic art.

Herbert's own art, in poems of meditation, lies partly in the subtle transformations and re-orderings of the accepted technique that come naturally to him. But this group of poems, these 'acts of pure attention' to the themes, incidents and mysteries of his faith, are explorations within this tradition. In one or two, like the sombre and prolonged *The Sacrifice*, we are more aware of imaginative 'composition', and subtle probings and graspings by the understanding, than of decisions of the will. It is because such realizations as these induce a grief and penitence that need no explicit moral injunction. In others, like *Prayer*, the composition is swiftly etched in, and the efforts to understand rightly, and live and act appropriately, dominate. We do best, perhaps, to see the tradition of meditation as no more than scaffolding; to unfold that aspect of the poems is not the same as to respond sensitively to what they say, and are. But it may help.

The comparable poems by others, chosen to end this section, very differently directed though they are, have two things in common. They are all three, it is not too much to affirm, supremely fine poems, among the finest of the age. And all three make pointed—and marvellously *creative*—use of the structure of meditation. The last poem of all, *To His Coy Mistress*, makes an appropriate end, for it is by way of suggesting a beginning, too. It is, at least ostensibly, secular poetry and not divine poetry at all; it takes its stand in the tradition of love poetry. But for the better and more powerful statement of its inner theme, Marvell applies both the dialectic of the rhetorician, and the meditation of the religious, to his courtly matter. (We recall how much of Herbert's skill lay in a kind of sacred parody of secular love poetry, especially Sidney's.) With *To His Coy Mistress* the reader is lured towards another world in seventeenth-century poetry, one (many would say) even more rewarding than Herbert's: and a new start must be made, with the *Songs and Sonnets* of Donne.

The poem *Aaron* has been chosen to stand first among the poems of this group because, in ways the reader may like to identify, it draws together skills and interests we have especially concentrated upon in earlier groups. A word or two of more detailed discussion of *The Agonie* may be better in place in this commentary. For *The Agonie* extends our appreciation towards a Herbert whose creative gift can encompass profound feeling and understanding, and a nervous force of declaration that has personal distress in it. It is said often that we live, now, in a time when our understanding and mastery of material nature has developed far beyond our understanding and mastery of ourselves, our moral being. The call to meditate which opens this poem is offered with something of that sense about it. Herbert presents the natural philosophers (the scientists of his day) not ironically, but with due respect, as authors of a kind of knowledge that has outmeasured our knowledge of our hearts, and our deep passions. Due respect: for is there not the weight of massive achievement in the first lines? Yet the third line does touch in a quip-like hint that with so much knowledge may come an overweening pride and self-confidence. Those measuring-rods that gauge the heights of the universe do not in fact take the human spirit in a pleasant walk to heaven; his danger is that he may suppose they do.

The moral realities remain, *Sinne* and *Love*; and in Christian faith they are tragically connected. To sound and measure these, to understand them, and, by understanding, to check and affect the will, is the meditative purpose in the poem. Herbert's art is directed to all possible vividness of 'composition', and to all possible strenuousness of 'understanding'. The end-result, the conforming of the will, remains unexpressed. For, traditionally, to meditate the nature and consequences of sin was taken to involve contrition, and an inward detestation carried with it a natural adjustment of desire and will. We can finely observe the rôle that active sense-experience plays at the behest of imagination, when the scene of Gethsemane, and the scene of Calvary, are summoned to consciousness. Gethsemane is tactual and physical:

> A man so wrung with pains, that all his hair,
>   His skinne, his garments bloudie be.
> Sinne is that presse and vice, which forceth pain
> To hunt his cruell food through ev'ry vein.

Calvary, more strangely, but in preparation for the poem's climax, tastes upon the tongue, and still retains the tactual sense of blood on the skin, and then again releases other sense-impressions with the liquid gush from the side of Christ. Such fusion of extreme susceptibility in sense-experience with passionate acts of thought has often been described as the essence of the 'metaphysical' style in poetry. And so it is; but behind it there is this older tradition, this act of pure but intense attention to the theme in hand. Behind Herbert's personal and original use, here, of the wine-press image, is a long history, pictorial, literary, and expository of scripture, of the application of that image to the Passion.

For a meditation that would 'know sinne', Gethsemane has a special fittingness as a focal point; it is there that sin has an 'unmeasurable' character, is felt as bodily anguish, and yet as so much more. 'The reader's understanding of the agony of knowledge; of the injustice and blindness of the bad men now approaching; of the uncaring sleep of the good ones; of the impending betrayal and the unpitied pain—his understanding of all that is involved in this especial example, is drawn upon to make the concepts presented more subtle.' (R. Tuve.) The second verse, then, composes an image that thoroughly sensitizes the consciousness to sin. The third reveals what sin calls forth, and what can defeat sin itself; and, at the same time, the image composed brings home what sin did to Love, and does still. That is the intricate connection binding into one the two stanzas, just as the predominating tactile feeling (from 'His sweat was as it were great drops of blood') binds them. Consider especially the last lines. The side of the pierced Christ is *set again abroach*. And with that phrase the poem, as it were, becomes whole. First, the painful but remedial flow from the pierced side acts to release an ease, a relief, into the poem's movement, lasting from there to the middle of the final line. Second, with *taste the like*, the implications of the Sacrament and the communion table, deep-set within the unfolding pattern of the poem, become clear at last. Third, Herbert's own readers would have recognized, and we should now, that the gravity and special point of this meditation on these themes originate in its being a 'Meditation before receiving the Sacrament': the theme, among those recommended for that preparation and penitence. The wine-press, the bloody skin, the pierced side, the winecask set abroach, partake now in confident affirmation of the Love which presides at the communion table.

Not that the affirmation is or can be a simple one. The last line divides: a half for Gethsemane, and sin; a half for Calvary, for Love, and for the present Sacrament. The Lord of Love is again for a moment, in the Garden, 'made sin for us', suffering the consequences of sin: *Which my God feels as bloud*. The line abruptly breaks off, with the sense of overwhelming mystery, and generosity, and with the humbling approach to the Sacrament itself: *but I, as wine*. To the last, things are felt, tasted: the tactile sense remains energetic, 'composing' the detail and the scene as vividly as devotion can enable, and poetic power can secure.

Notes

AARON

A meditation on true priesthood, turning not only upon Aaron's rôle as the type of the priest, but, as the understanding fastens upon the significance of the 'composition', on Christ as the great High Priest. 'I live, yet not I, but Christ lives in me' provides the essential clue to the poem's growth.

'Each verse of the poem suggests metrically the swelling and dying sound of a bell; and, like a bell, the rhymes reiterate the same sound.' Grierson's suggestion reminds us with what feeling for the pattern, the rhymes, and the images, we need to attend. But perhaps his interpretation does less for the stationary rhyme-words than the poem requires. They seem to hold tenaciously there the rôle of the ideal priest. One after another the aspirants to it possess the verses—Aaron, Herbert, Christ, Herbert-in-Christ and Christ-in-Herbert. The outer garments do not change, only the inward possessor.

Holinesse on the head . . . traditionally the garments of Aaron had come to symbolize aspects of true priesthood. *Exodus* xxviii. provides the starting-point. Aaron's mitre there has a gold plate engraved with the words 'Holiness to the Lord'; his breastplate contains 'the Lights and Perfections'; pomegranates and bells alternate at the hem of his robe.

Harmonious bells below, raising the dead . . . bells had come to symbolize the preacher's voice proclaiming the Gospel. But Herbert's use of them through this poem includes that further play of suggestion—their *chimes*—we have met before. The second verse needs study in this light. Note that by the third verse the bells have become 'musick' itself.

My onely musick, striking me ev'n dead . . . *striking* is used both in the apparent sense ('I am dead, and my life is hid with Christ'); and to give the striking of the bell by the clapper—with all those further suggestions of chiming order, spiritual harmony.

THE PULLEY

A meditation on the gifts of God. The act of understanding forges the clarities of the third stanza.

Rest in the bottome lay . . . the play upon the word, from its associations with Primero, haunts the verses that follow. The reader should consult the glossary, and reflect, too, on the more familiar meanings of the word.

PRAYER (II)

That state dislikes not easinesse . . . *state*, here, means high estate, courtly eminence. The *easinesse* subtly brings together the notion of free access, and of unselfconscious grace and ease of manner: the opposite of artificial deference, of obsequiousness. The reader will by now have noticed, from *The Collar*, *Affliction (I)* and other poems, how constantly, as a quiet image of reference, Herbert presents the relationship of the faithful soul to God under the figure of courtier to noble or to King.

Tacks the centre to the sphere . . . 'The sphere, the apparent outward limit of space, is at all points equidistant from its centre, the earth.' (Canon Hutchinson.)

To take our flesh and curse . . . Relate to *Galatians*, iii. 13.

THE AGONIE

Observe the relationship between the last line of the first stanza and of the last. Is it, perhaps, this brokenness in the final couplets on either side that makes the harsh force of the final couplet in the middle stanza doubly grim?

THE SACRIFICE

'Herbert's *Sacrifice* is a *meditation* upon the liturgy, developing the events of Passion Week according to the intricate methods of the seventeenth century: visualization, intellectual analysis, profit drawn from the dual and simultaneous vision of the God made man. . . . The central aim of the art of meditation was to make explicit whatever remained implicit in the medieval heritage: to analyse, to understand, and then to feel and profit from the matter. This is exactly the difference we feel between Herbert's subtle, deft, explicit treatment of the paradoxes, and the simple, implicit statement of the paradoxes which one finds in the liturgy and in popular medieval poetry.' (L. Martz.)

Professor Martz's admirable summary of the nature of the poem directs attention to the wrong kind of emphasis upon the traditional character of its methods, symbols, and paradoxes in Rosamund Tuve's long study of *The Sacrifice* in *A Reading of George Herbert*. The proviso once entered, however, there is a good deal to be learnt from Miss Tuve's account.

Together with Professor Martz's pages, no student of *The Sacrifice* should miss Empson's analysis in *Seven Types of Ambiguity*. And it may be said that nothing but a careful, energetic *study* will do any justice to *The Sacrifice*. The reader should be aware how deeply embedded in Christian folk poetry and liturgy the whole style is: the creation of a monologue for the suffering Christ is not Herbert's invention. Starting in the quotation from the *Lamentations of Jeremiah*, 'Is it nothing to you, all ye that pass by?' such monologues, albeit far shorter, belong with the most ancient Passion services of the Church. The ironies and paradoxes themselves are many of them ancient. But Herbert, throughout, is re-creating, re-fashioning, possessing inwardly, exploring, and, as a poet, 'making his own' the tragic and paradoxical conceptions.

'In *The Sacrifice*, with a magnificence he never excelled, the various sets of conflicts in the Christian doctrine of the Sacrifice are stated with an assured and easy simplicity, a reliable and unassuming grandeur, extraordinary in any material, but unique as achieved by successive fireworks of contradiction, and a mind jumping like a flea.' (Empson.)

Who never thought that any robberie . . . It would be rewarding to look up *Philippians* ii. and to study the opening of the chapter, not merely as supplying the thought here, but as an example of the style of paradox inherent in the Christian tradition.

He clave the stonie rock . . . the tone is ironic: Caesar, then, is their Moses.

They buffet him . . . Canon Hutchinson suggests that the sudden change to the third person 'heightens the insolence of the soldiers in maltreating one who is the ruler of the universe'. But it is not a true transition; Christ Himself remains, clearly, the speaker.

That he before me well nigh suffereth . . . 'so violently they shout (shouting their *utmost*) as nearly to give out their last (utmost) breath, and so die before me.'

The earths great curse in Adams fall . . . that brought thorns upon the earth.

My crosse I bear my self . . . Empson's account of the poem, valuable all through, is especially stimulating when these stanzas are discussed.

But sharper that confound . . . reproaches pierce the soul, reproaches such as that of the next stanza.

That as sinne came, so Sacraments might flow . . . the first woman, and the consequent tragedy of the Fall, came from the side of Adam.

Henry King's THE EXEQUY

Born in 1592, the son of a bishop, Henry King was ordained at Oxford, and became a canon at Christ Church. He was made bishop of Chichester in 1642, ejected the next year, and restored to his See at the Restoration. He died in 1669. He had been a friend of Donne and many other writers; his poems—they were not many, nor was poetry a major part of his life—appeared anonymously after his death. That so moving and beautiful a poem as *The Exequy* could come from the hand of a minor poet suggests something of the strength of the tradition King shared.

He had married Anne Berkeley in 1617, and seven years later, still young, she died. The drama of the poem lies partly in its endeavour to compose a formal meditation upon the holy death of his wife, an endeavour which again and again breaks down before the actuality of his grief and loss.

The piercing wit, the naturally light and mobile metre, and the constantly interrupted meditative structure, serve alike to give the poem a control and grace matched, but not excelled, by Herbert or Marvell at their greatest.

John Donne's GOODFRIDAY, 1613: RIDING WESTWARD

The manuscript headings give us 'Riding to Sir Edward Herbert in Wales', and 'Mr. J. Donne, goeing from Sir H. G. on good friday sent him back this meditation on the way'.

Shorter though it is, this meditation makes a valuable comparison with Herbert's *The Sacrifice*. In what way is it more 'personal'? How would one distinguish the intellectual energy at work in the two poems?

The first ten lines form an elaborate, very carefully contrived 'composition by similitude'. The problem is established: profane motives carry the soul away from God, while the soul's essence, devotion, longs for Him. By intellectual analysis, the paradox of human perversity is developed. Going westward on business, Donne is refusing to perform the devotion proper to the day, refusing to *see* the place, and participate in its agony as if he were really present. Yet in the very act of saying he does not see these things, he develops their significance. The last ten lines provide the colloquy and the will's resolves are made.

Andrew Marvell's TO HIS COY MISTRESS

There are more important sides to this wonderful poem, but the meditative structure comes out as clearly as does the If–But–Therefore dialectic of the argument. A 'composition' upon the coy lady leads to an 'understanding' of the truths of the situation, and this to a 'resolve' of the will.

Marvell's suggestions of a more serious undercurrent may be felt by the alert reader well before the tremendous change in style and movement that comes with the second section. What, for example, really *is* 'the last Age'?

Does the remarkable power of the final section depend in some measure upon this fusion between gaiety and urgent seriousness —meditative resolution directed upon the fulfilment of a love relationship?

Suggestions for Further Reading

POETRY

The Metaphysical Poets (edited Helen Gardner) Penguin
Poems of Sidney ('Silver Poets of the 16th century') Everyman
Donne: The Divine Poems (edited Helen Gardner) O.U.P.
The Works of Donne (edited John Hayward) Nonesuch Press
**The Works of Herbert* (edited F. E. Hutchinson) O.U.P.
The Temple & *The Priest to the Temple* Everyman
(a more modestly priced text of Herbert's
complete work in prose and verse)
Andrew Marvell: Poetry & Prose (L.L.L. Library) Harrap
The Poems of Vaughan (Muse's Library) Routledge

BIOGRAPHY

**The Lives of Donne, Wotton, Hooker, Herbert & Sanderson*, by Walton. World's Classics
George Herbert, by Margaret Bottrall. Murray
(with some valuable discussion of his work)

CRITICISM

*'George Herbert' in *Explorations*, by L. C. Knights. Chatto
*'The Line of Wit' in *Revaluation*, by F. R. Leavis. Chatto
**The Poetry of Meditation*, by Louis Martz. O.U.P.
George Herbert, his religion and art, by J. H. Summers. Chatto
A Reading of George Herbert, by R. Tuve. Faber
Four Metaphysical Poets, by J. Bennett. C.U.P.
*'The Metaphysical Poets' and 'Andrew Marvell' in *Selected Essays*, by T. S. Eliot. Faber
**Seven Types of Ambiguity* (parts), by W. Empson. Chatto
Music and Poetry of the English Renaissance, by B. Pattison. Methuen
From Donne to Marvell, ed. B. Ford (Penguin Guide to English Literature). Penguin

*The more essential aids to study

Glossary

This glossary has been compiled simply for working purposes. Some words appear precisely in the grammatical usage of a poem in which they may give difficulty; others in generic form. Making the glossary easy to consult, and elusive words easy to trace, has been the only rule. Some words appear only because their seventeenth-century spelling may at first disguise them from the unpractised eye. Frequently the gloss against a word serves the reading of the poems in this book only, and is far from exhaustive even for that. Where a familiar word still current is used with some play upon a second meaning now less familiar, the glossary draws attention only to the less familiar meaning. Where a word is used more than once in the poems, and in varying senses, the full range of meanings is given, and the reader will judge how much of the possible sense has relevance to one particular usage. It is always worth bearing in mind, however, that writers of this period rarely use a word without at least being alert to all its possible meanings, even if no deliberate play upon different meanings is intended. A comma separates words that are meant to amplify one line of suggestion, and a semi-colon separates distinct meanings. The glossary is of course no more than a sketchy *start* to the exploration of Herbert's handling of words. It has nothing like the adequacy of a good dictionary. If the editor's insufficiency, or apparently arbitrary readings, send the irritated reader to a dictionary, a really useful purpose will have been served.

Abjects   Downtrodden people; the degraded and hopeless
Abroach   Pierced to let liquid flow
Ado   Trouble; business

Adventuring   Faring forth on a venture; undertaking a risk
Afford   Furnish with; manage to spare
Almanake   Almanach
Angell   Guardian angel; coin with device of St. Michael on it
Angrie   (of colour) flushed red, like a face flushed in anger
Antiphon   Composition of passages said or sung in alternation by voices or groups of voices, in worship
Antipodes   Furthest-known regions of earth; place most totally opposed to 'here'
Assay   Make trial; test the purity of metals; attempt what is difficult
Audit   Render account of
Augment   Increase

Balsome   Balsam, healing lotion
Bands   Bonds; groups of people banded or bound together
Barre   Bar; barrier
Bayes   Wreath of bay leaves
Bead   Prayer; one of a set of beads for 'telling' prayers, to ensure completeness
Benighted   Overtaken by darkness; out at night
Bent   Intent upon; set towards; curved
Benumme   Make numb
Besett'st   Surround or support on all sides; encompass
Bill   Halberd, spear and battle-axe combined
Bloud   Blood
Bloudie   Bloody
Blouds   Flushes up with blood; fills with rising blood
Bottom   Ship
Brackish   Dank; unwholesome; long standing
Brave   Finely dressed; superb; courageous; forthright
Bridall   Wedding festivity (bride—ale)
Burnish   Grow in vigour and strength; spread out; polish by friction

Calcine   Burn to ashes; desiccate; refine by destroying grosser part
Canker   Infect with ulcerous disease
Censorious   Apt to blame or find fault
Centrie   Sentry; one of a band
Chair   Chair of state; bier; portable carriage like an eastern rickshaw
Chargd   Accused of; filled with
Chast   Chaste; pure
Chime   Rhyme; sound in time together
Clause   Single proviso (as in a treaty); complete and conclusive utterance (note Latin derivation)

Clear   Remove obstruction; free from obligation by paying dues; establish innocence
Cleare   Open, frank, innocent
Clerer   Clearer
Clime   Tract of country
Closes   Cadences; chords that end a musical phrase
Cockatrice   Fabulous creature hatched by a serpent from a cock's egg: its breath was thought to kill
Combind   Bound together into unity
Comments   Commentary; full exposition
Commodities   Articles for sale or barter
Compacted   Condensed close together
Complaint   Formal verses of grief
Compute   Add up
Constraint   Compulsion
Contrarieties   Oppositions in nature; tensions; inconsistencies
Convert   Cause to return after straying; cause a change of heart
Cops   Copse, coppice, little underwood
Cordiall   Medicine to stimulate the heart; heart-restoring (as adjective)
Cordially   From the heart, with warmth
Corrections   Punishments
Count   Take full account of; assess exactly
Course-spunne   Rough in texture, unskilled in weave
Coy   Modest; negative; shy in such a way as to allure
Crosse-bias   Give an involuntary inclination, against nature (from the game of bowls)
Curl   Decorate (with a suggestion of aristocratic refinement); affected, or glamorous, self-adornment

Deare   Costly; beloved
Deaths head   Skull as emblem of mortality
Deck   Array, adorn; furnish with
Delicates   Delicacies pleasing to the senses; luxuries
Demean   Bearing, demeanour; estate or condition, demesne
Desert   Thing rightly deserved, properly owing
Desperation   Condition of total despair
Despitefulness   Spite mixed with derision
Disclaim   Abandon all claims; deny all responsibility
Dissent   Refuse to agree
Double   Deceiving; two-faced; twofold
Dutie   Obeisances; respects

Easie   Informal; natural; comfortable

Eies Eyes
Elements Earth, water, fire and air, taken as constituents of the human frame
Elixir Philosopher's Stone, supposed by the old Alchemists to change metals into gold; or thought of as infinitely prolonging life; figuratively, the sovereign remedy
Enroll Place on a roll of honour; celebrate by public witness
Enthrall Make a slave; captivate with delight
Equall Evenly balanced; justly proportioned
Extoll Lift up; raise aloft by due praise in public

Fence Bulwark; fortification; place of de-fence
Fiction Inventions; fanciful elaborations of fact; untruth; insincerity
Field Battlefield
Fit Space; episode; suitable; allowed
Flung away Hurried off in indignation
Foot To clutch with the claw
Forraigne Foreign; alien
Frame Ordered arrangement or disposition ('frame of mind'); related to an underlying structure
Free Unfettered; liberal
Furnisht Provided

Gains Positive worth; achievements; possessions
Gall Typical bitter substance (from bile, secretion of the liver)
Geere Jeer
Generall To all men in common; universal
Giddinesse Spinning or circling with bewildering speed, and its consequences; mental intoxication; inconstancy
Glide Slip gently away; pass unnoticed
Gon Gone
Grones Groans; sighs, laments

Hawk Hunt, with hawk for prey-catcher
Head Make a head, press forward in a body; fountain-head, source (noun)
Home Touching one on the quick; intimately (adverb)
Hony Honey
Houre Span of life; reminder of fleetingness of time; urgency

Impale Transfix (a body) as on a stake; fence in with stakes
Increase Add wealth; harvest what has been sown; growth, harvest (noun)

Indure   Endure
Ingrosse   Concentrate the whole in one
Intelligence   Directing mind
Interest   Acquired right of possession; concern
Interpose   Place between
Invention   Creation of the mind; subject matter (as opposed to 'style')

Large   On the grand scale; at large; at length
Light   Serenity of heart; brightness
Lines   Directions; ship's ropes; verses; and as suggested in the modern colloquialism, 'What's his line?'
List   Care to; wish to
Liveries   Uniforms of servants of the nobility
Lowre   Lour, look dark upon

Maladies   Ailments or illnesses of body or soul
Manour   Manor house; Hall
Measure   Be equal in measure with; commensurate with
Medow   Meadow
Miserable   Much to be pitied
Missery   Misery, with suggestion of having missed (lost the way, lost contact with the guide)
Moldeth   Moulds
Moneth   Month
Move   Prompt; incline; affect with emotion; keep in motion

Noise   A band of musicians
Note   Perceive; take note of

Offring at   Aiming towards
Onely   Only (note the emphasis, *one-ly*)
Optick   Telescope

Palsy   Paralysis
Parcell   Item (of an inventory); part (of an estate)
Partie   Conspiracy; faction
Paschal   Of the Passover
Passing-bell   Funeral bell
Perfection   Completeness; faultlessness; highest pitch of excellence
Physick   Medicine
Pink   Stab home; pierce with sword point or foil (as in fencing)
Plate   Royal dish (as 'silver plate')

Precedence   Going before
Prefixt   Ordained beforehand; or (as in the modern colloquialism) 'fixed'
Prepossest   Given a prior claim; first possession
Preposterous   Contrary to nature; absurd
Presse   Wine-press; printing-press
Prethee   Prithee: 'I pray thee'
Prime   First, or 'prime Player' in Primero (a gambling game with cards); hour of the early morning Office of the Church
Pull   Draw (in cards)
Pulley   Mechanical device for directing, re-directing or adjusting power
Purling   Flowing with whirling motion and bubbling sound

Quick   Alive; lively
Quickend   Brought to life; hasted
Quip   Neat provocative witticism or retort

Ragd   Ragged
Ranges   Strays far and wide; inconstant in thought and affection
Ravish   Violate; carry off by force; enchant with delight
Razd   Laid level with the ground
Receit   Medical prescription; recipe
Relish   Take delight in taste; please the other senses; sweet tastes and flavours (noun)
Remove   Move off; move away again
Rendereth   Gives back; sends back
Repair   Betake oneself somewhere
Repining   Fretting discontentedly, not for the first time
Reprove   Endure again (re-prove); rebuke
Resigning   Self-denial; renunciation (resignation)
Rest   Stake; what one stands to win or lose at Primero (see *Prime* above)
Rheume   Feverish chill; infection
Rode   Road, highway
Rout   Mob
Rudely   In the state of nature; untrained; coarse; rough-and-ready; lacking sensitiveness and perception

Savour   Taste; perception
Scrue   Screw (possibly 'screw-driver' also)
Seal'd   Closed securely; the eyelids sewn up (seeling a hawk); figuratively, hoodwinked
Season'd   Matured by exposure, habituation and growth

Secure Make fast
Sed Said
Set Sunset; dusk
Set me light Make light of me; despise and deride
Severall Distinct and separate
Shadie Shadowed; darkened
Shrouds Covers, as for burial
Shrowd Garment for the dead
Silly Simple, naive, innocent
Simpring Feigned and acquiescent smiling
Slow-chapt With slowly masticating jaws
Smart Sharp, stinging pain
Snudge Remain snug and quiet; be stingy in solitude
Sort Result, turn out so; to work out so, as by luck
Sowre Sour
Spacious Composed of vast spaces
Spare Be thrifty; be sparing by habit, or sparing of expense
Sped Successful ('God speed you')
Spend Expend, give out
Spight Spite
Spirit To inspirit, fill with the spirit
Staffe Staff; measuring rod
State High standing; high estate
Stemme Deflect; fight against; seek to halt
Subsist Keep alive, keep life present in; uphold
Subtill Subtle; mysterious; pervasive; cunning; undermining
Sudden Appearing unexpectedly; impulsive
Suit Do service to; official request, favour (noun); be under contract of service ('in suit')
Sweet Fragrant; pleasant; fresh; sound; beloved; lovable
Sweets Perfumes
Symphony Harmony; consonance of ordered sounds; prelude

Tack Fasten; secure
Temper'd Prepared by moistening, mixing and kneading (of clay); blended
Then Than (frequently spelt thus)
Thrall Bondage, servitude
Thrust into Push oneself forward into; drive ambitiously towards
Till Money-drawer
Tincture Spiritual principle whose quality could be infused into material things (in alchemy); dye (see Latin derivation)
Told Assessed; counted up

Touch Test the standard and quality of gold by rubbing with touchstone
Train-bands Trained bands (a sort of civil defence unit); figuratively, a group of adherents, properly trained
Transpire Emit, like perspiration, through pores of skin
Trimmed Garbed; prepared for journey; excellently turned out
Tune To put in tune (of an instrument); join in harmony with
Turn Need; purpose (as in 'serve his turn')
Twist Cord made of silk fibres wound round one another
Type A definite emblem or symbol, fixed in its reference

Unbridled Unrestrained; uncontrolled; with the bridle off (specially used of the appetites and desires)
Uncouth Awkward; unmannerly; unexpected; comfortless
Untimely By no means due; out of turn; unprepared for

Vain Given to vanity; empty; bewildering; to no purpose
Vann Vanguard; those in front of the battle lines
Vegetable Plant-like; apt for growth; able to reproduce
Vent Utter forth; discharge; sell
Ventilate Increase flame by fanning or blowing
Viall Small jar, usually for medicines
Vies Contests, struggles

Wave Waver; waive, declining an offer or not asserting a right
Weal Welfare; blessedness
Weed Clothing
Whitt Least particle
Wide Wide of the mark; astray; empty of meaning
Wilde Desert; desolate place
Wink Remain blind to; keep eyes closed; sleep
Wold Open uncultivated moorland (*would*, signifying will-power or desire, was pronounced the same way)
Working Active, full of effort; fermenting, like yeast; agitated
Wrastling Wrestling

Zenith Point of utmost height above the observer; opposite to; infinite point away from
Zone The Torrid Zone, area of intense heat

© Douglas Brown 1960